DK EYEWITNESS

T0043314

TOP 10
VANCOUVER
AND VANCOUVER ISLAND

Top 10 Vancouver and Vancouver Island Highlights

The Top 10 of Everything

CONTENTS

Vancouver and Vancouver Island Area by Area

Streetsmart

Within each Top 10 list in this book, no hierarchy of quality or popularity is implied. All ten are, in the editor's opinion, of roughly equal merit.

Throughout this book, floors are referred to in accordance with American usage; i.e., the "first floor" is at ground level.

Title page, front cover and spine
Picturesque Vancouver skyline against North Shore mountains
Back cover, clockwise from top left *Long Beach at sunset; Downtown Vancouver; Gastown's iconic Steam Clock; Vancouver skyline; Stanley Park Seawall along Burrard Inlet*

The rate at which the world is changing is constantly keeping the DK Eyewitness team on our toes. While we've worked hard to ensure that this edition of Vancouver and Vancouver Island is accurate and up-to-date, we know that opening hours alter, standards shift, prices fluctuate, places close and new ones pop up in their stead. So, if you notice we've got something wrong or left something out, we want to hear about it. Please get in touch at **travelguides@dk.com**

Welcome to
Vancouver and Vancouver Island

A city of gleaming skyscrapers surrounded by ocean and snow-capped mountains, Vancouver features world-class art galleries and museums, stunning green spaces, and an exciting food scene. A short journey away, Vancouver Island offers scenic towns along the coastline. With DK Eyewitness Top 10 Vancouver and Vancouver Island, it's yours to explore.

The Waterfront and Downtown districts are likely to be your first introduction to the city of Vancouver; some outstanding attractions are nestled near glitzy **Canada Place**, including **Vancouver Lookout**, **Christ Church Cathedral**, **Vancouver Art Gallery**, and **Science World**. Nearby, a 6-mile (9-km) waterfront path meanders around the edges of **Stanley Park**, a rare urban wilderness with incredible vistas. More attractions await on the city's south shore, including the sprawling **Vanier Park**, home to the **H. R. MacMillan Space Centre** and a few museums, while **Granville Island** hosts a vibrant Public Market.

Beyond the city, Greater Vancouver features **Capilano Suspension Bridge Park**, as well as a mind-blowing array of outdoor pursuits in **Whistler**. With its wild coastline, **Vancouver Island** is also a popular outdoor destination. Its laid-back provincial capital **Victoria** hosts the **Royal BC Museum** and historic **Inner Harbour**.

Whether you're coming for a weekend or a week, our Top 10 guide brings together the best of everything the region has to offer, from the trendiest restaurants and bars to a year-round roster of festivals and events. The guide has useful tips throughout, from seeking out what's free to getting off the beaten path, plus seven easy-to-follow itineraries designed to tie together a clutch of sights in a short space of time. Add inspiring photography and detailed maps, and you've got the essential pocket-sized travel companion. **Enjoy the book, and enjoy Vancouver and Vancouver Island**.

Clockwise from top: **Detail of the sails at Canada Place**, Victoria's British Columbia Parliament Buildings, the Capilano Suspension Bridge in North Vancouver, Vancouver's skyscrapers, a totem pole in Stanley Park, ski slopes in Whistler, the sunken garden in Butchart Gardens

Exploring Vancouver and Vancouver Island

The city of Vancouver – buzzing with culture and a fabulous food scene – is surrounded by ocean, mountains and the Pacific rainforest, with stunning Vancouver Island just across the Georgia Strait. Here are a few ideas for your stay, whether you only have time for the must-see sights, or can explore Greater Vancouver and beyond.

The striking sail-like silhouette of Canada Place, built for Expo '86, is instantly recognizable.

Key
— Two-day itinerary
— Seven-day itinerary

Two Days in Vancouver

Day ❶

MORNING

Take a stroll around **Canada Place** (see pp14–15) to view the harbor. Jump on the SkyTrain at landmark Waterfront Station to explore the award-winning **Science World** (see pp26–7). Afterwards, sit for lunch in hip **Gastown** (see p69).

AFTERNOON

Check out either the much-loved **Vancouver Art Gallery** (see pp20–21) or the captivating **Bill Reid Gallery** (see p77), then window-shop on bustling **Robson Street** (see p76). Afterward, treat yourself to dinner or cocktails at one of the swanky downtown eateries (see p81).

Day ❷

MORNING

Rent a bike to explore the green lungs of the city, **Stanley Park** (see pp12–13), and visit its intriguing Aquarium. Follow the Seawall as it snakes around the edge of the park to take in views of Burrard Inlet and English Bay, and then ride the Aquabus to **Granville Island** (see pp24–5).

AFTERNOON

Delight in the local produce and handmade wares at **Granville Island Public Market** (see p86) and, if you have the energy, cycle on to the museums in **Vanier Park** (see p85), or head to **Sunset Beach** (see p83).

Granville Island Public Market sells an enticing array of fresh local produce.

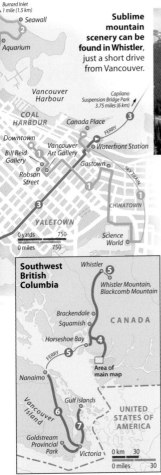

Sublime mountain scenery can be found in Whistler, just a short drive from Vancouver.

from the **Capilano Suspension Bridge** (see pp16–17). Afterwards, return to the city, where 20 minutes from downtown, Northwest Coast First Nations art and culture is celebrated at the unparalleled **Museum of Anthropology at UBC** (see pp18–19). Combine your visit with a walking tour of the campus.

Day ❹
Set off on the 75-mile (120-km) drive to **Whistler** (see pp34–5) on the Sea-to-Sky Highway (Hwy 99), taking in adventure-sports paradise **Squamish** (see p102) and the small town of **Brackendale** (see p103) en route.

Day ❺
Explore Whistler Village and ride the gondola up Whistler Mountain where you'll find picturesque trails and the PEAK 2 PEAK gondola to Blackcomb Mountain for superb alpine sightseeing. Drive down to Horseshoe Bay in West Vancouver for the ferry to **Nanaimo** (see p94).

Day ❻
After exploring Nanaimo's Old Quarter, make a beeline for provincial capital **Victoria** (see pp28–9). Here, take in the city's Inner Harbour and the outstanding **Royal BC Museum** (see pp30–31).

Day ❼
Dedicate your final day to the great outdoors. Hike in old-growth rain forest at **Goldstream Provincial Park** (see p94), try a whale-watching tour, or head to the **Gulf Islands** (see p93).

Seven Days in Vancouver and Vancouver Island

Days ❶ and ❷
Follow the activities in the two-day Vancouver itinerary.

Day ❸
Take the SeaBus from Waterfront Station to Lonsdale Quay and its market in **North Vancouver** (see p102). Don't miss the West Coast rain forest and the dizzying views

Top 10 Vancouver and Vancouver Island Highlights

Canada Place and Vancouver
Waterfront at dusk

Vancouver and Vancouver Island Highlights

Poised between the Pacific Ocean and the Coast Mountain range, Vancouver is one of the most beautifully located cities on earth. With a lively cultural scene and great restaurants, it is often listed among the world's best places to live. A short ferry ride away, Victoria is a great base from which to explore the many natural wonders of Vancouver Island.

1 Stanley Park
Created in 1888, Stanley Park is North America's third-largest urban park. It offers a heady mix of forest and ocean (see pp12–13).

2 Canada Place
Built for Expo '86, Canada Place is an outstanding convention and hotel complex overlooking Vancouver Harbour. Cruise ships dock alongside an inviting promenade (see pp14–15).

3 Capilano Suspension Bridge Park
Teeter over a wooden bridge high above the Capilano River, walk along a boardwalk into the treetops, and learn about local history, forest ecology, and Indigenous culture at this incredible park (see pp16–17).

4 Museum of Anthropology at UBC
This museum houses one of the world's finest displays of Northwest Coast First Nations arts. The European ceramics and textiles are also a highlight (see pp18–19).

5 Vancouver Art Gallery
From the swirling forests of BC artist Emily Carr to radical installations, this gallery features the best of West Coast and international art (see pp20–21).

Lost Lagoon

Devonian Harbour Park

COAL HARBOUR

COMOX STREET

DENMAN STREET

WEST GEORGIA STREET

WEST PEND STREET

WEST END

Alexandra Park

BEACH AVENUE

DAVIE STREET

BARCLAY STREET

NICOLA STREET

COMOX STREET

JERVIS STREET

DOWNTOWN

THURLOW STREET

DAVIE VILLAGE

PACIFIC STREET

BURRARD STREET

HOWE STREET

English Bay

Vanier Park

6 miles (9 km)

Davie Lam Park

False

Around Vancouver

6 Granville Island

This popular peninsula on False Creek is a bustling mix of shops, galleries, restaurants, and theaters (see pp24–5).

7 Science World

Science comes alive inside the dome-shaped Science World. Hands-on exhibits inspire and capture the imaginations of all ages (see pp26–7).

8 Victoria

With its historic buildings and green parks, Victoria makes a great base for trips around Vancouver Island (see pp28–9).

9 Around Tofino

Wild Pacific shores, rare old-growth forests and spectacular scenery abound in the Tofino area on Vancouver Island's rugged west coast (see pp32–3).

Whistler 10

Ideally placed for a city escape, Whistler is an upscale resort a two-hour drive north from Vancouver. Two mountains tower over alpine-style resort villages. Skiers abound here but there are countless other year-round activities (see pp34–5).

TOP 10 ⭐ Stanley Park

A local favorite with a rich history, spectacular Stanley Park is a mere ten-minute bus ride from downtown. Forest walks, beachside strolls, and a vibrant rose garden are among its natural attractions. Activities include a children's water park, playgrounds, tennis courts, and a pitch-and-putt course. Located inside the park, the Vancouver Aquarium is world-renowned for its realistic walk-through exhibits based on scientific research projects. To the north of the park lies the iconic Lions Gate Bridge, designated a National Historic Site of Canada. Two Art Deco lion sculptures guard its entrance.

1 Lost Lagoon
A wildlife sanctuary, this willow-fringed lagoon (**above**) protects a bevy of wood ducks, blue herons, and white swans.

2 Siwash Rock
According to Squamish legend, this ancient lava rock deposit jutting up from the water was an Indigenous warrior who turned to stone.

4 Rose Garden
A formal rose garden blossoms year-round. From June to October, a variety of perennial plantings ensure vibrant color.

THE HISTORY OF STANLEY PARK
Home to Coast Salish communities for thousands of years before Europeans arrived, the peninsula was used by colonialists as a military reserve because of its strategic position. It was established as a city park in 1888, dedicated to Governor General Stanley. To stop erosion, the Seawall was built in 1917.

3 Seawall
Pedestrians, cyclists, and joggers happily share the 6-mile (9-km) paved path ringing the park (**below**), with its unimpeded views of English Bay and Burrard Inlet. Look out for the sculpture *Girl in a Wetsuit* on an offshore rock.

Prospect Point ⑤

Set on the northern tip of the peninsula, this is the park's highest point. It affords unrivaled views of the striking Lions Gate Bridge, built across the dark-blue Burrard Inlet **(right)**, with the magnificent Coast Mountains in the backdrop.

⑥ Brockton Point Visitor Centre

Carved gateways and a cedarwood interpretive pavilion welcome visitors. One of the poles on display is a carved copy of a pre-1878 Skedans mortuary pole by Haida artist Bill Reid.

⑨ Brockton Point

The point offers a terrific view of Burrard Inlet. In 1915, a lighthouse was built to guide vessels into the harbor. Sailors set their chronometers by the Nine-O'Clock Gun at the nearby Hallelujah Point. Its boom has been heard nightly since 1894.

⑩ Vancouver Aquarium

Marine displays capture the drama of the West Coast. Sea otters, rays, penguins, jellyfish **(below)** and several other sea creatures from around the globe can be seen at this aquarium.

Stanley Park

⑧ ⑤ ③ ⑩
⑨

PARK DRIVE
STANLEY PARK DRIVE
PIPE LINE RD
CAUSEWAY
Burrard Inlet
NORTH LAGOON DR
Coal Harbour
Deadman's Island
ℹ
WEST GEORGIA ST
ROBSON ST
LAGOON DRIVE

② ⑦ ① ④ ⑥

⑦ English Bay

The sandy beaches at the bay draw crowds. Sunbathers relax against driftwood logs at Third Beach, and the heated saltwater pool at Second Beach offers a warmer alternative to the bay.

⑧ Beaver Lake

Hiking trails to Beaver Lake follow old logging roads through a forest. Frogs, raccoons, coyotes, and rabbits may be spotted at the natural-state lake fringed by cattails and water lilies.

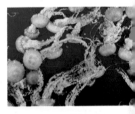

NEED TO KNOW

MAP G1 ■ 311
■ www.vancouver.ca

Main Park: open 6am–10pm (washrooms open dawn–dusk)

Vancouver Aquarium: 845 Avison Way; 778 655 9554; open 9:30am–5:30pm daily; adm adult $39.95–$51.95, seniors and students $35.20 and up, children $25.20 and up, under-3s free; book tickets online in advance: www.vanaqua.org

■ There are many restaurants throughout the park, with three food outlets at the Aquarium.

■ Traffic in the park is one way (counterclockwise)

and parking fees are strictly enforced.

■ It's a good idea to rent a bicycle. Hire from Spokes Bicycle Rentals *(1798 W Georgia St; www.spokes bicyclerentals.com)* nearby.

■ Bus tours and numerous hiking trails provide ways to explore all corners of the park.

TOP 10 ⭐ Canada Place

Built for Expo '86 as the flagship Canada Pavilion, Canada Place is a Vancouver landmark. The roof's futuristic sail-like lines echo Canada's nautical roots. The "prow" extends well into the harbor. Following the highly successful world exhibition, which attracted more than 22 million visitors, Canada Place was transformed into a complex containing a cruise-ship terminal, a convention center, exhibition areas, a flight simulation ride, and a first-class hotel. The promenade offers a terrific view of the city's harbor.

1 Architecture
Built for Expo '86 on the site of a former cargo dock, Canada Place's award-winning design is notable for its five Teflon-coated fiberglass sails, resembling a sailing ship **(above)**.

2 Destination Vancouver Visitor Desk
Operated by Destination Vancouver, this useful bureau, located in the Convention Centre East, offers free brochures and city maps. Volunteers can be seen outside the building wearing blue vests.

3 The Canadian Trail
The trail **(below)** is a walk through Canadian history. Interactive exhibits highlight Canada's heritage, innovations, sports, and geography. The walkway also offers great views of Stanley Park and the North Shore Mountains.

4 Vancouver Convention Centre
This state-of-the-art, eco-designed facility **(above)** has a landscaped, gray-water-irrigated "living roof," the largest in Canada, and is home to thousands of honey bees and over two dozen native plant species.

7 Community Events

Canada Place hosts various events **(left)**, including free yoga and zumba classes, busker performances, light displays, and film screenings.

5 Port Metro Vancouver's Discovery Centre

Located at the north end of Canada Place, this center educates visitors about the port through interactive touchscreen kiosks, videos, and presentations.

EXPO '86

On May 2 1986, Prince Charles and Princess Diana opened Expo '86, an immensely successful international fair. The event unfortunately closed with a deficit of $311 million. However, enduring legacies, such as Canada Place, Science World, the SkyTrain, and the urban renewal of False Creek, show that Expo '86 ultimately gave back a great deal to the people of Vancouver.

9 Cruise Ship Terminal

A three-berth cruise ship terminal is adjacent to the promenade at Canada Place, and welcomes hundreds of thousands of visitors a year. From the terminal, it's a short walk to the sights and shops of Gastown *(see p69)*.

6 Heritage Horns

Every day, at noon, the sound of ten air horns blasts across Vancouver from the top of Canada Place. Designed and built by Robert Swanson in 1967 as a project to celebrate Canada's 100th birthday, the first four notes of the chimes are from the national anthem, *O Canada*.

8 Floatplanes

Pontooned planes **(above)** from Victoria land at Coal Harbour, west of Canada Place. Helicopters from Victoria descend to the east of the complex.

10 FlyOver™ Canada

Visitors of all ages can soar from coast to coast on a breathtaking virtual journey that takes in the excitement and grandeur of Canada's landscape in the latest flight ride technology. Effects such as wind, sounds, and scents all add to the experience.

NEED TO KNOW

MAP L2 ■ 999 Canada Pl ■ 604 665 9000 ■ www.canadaplace.ca

Destination Vancouver Visitor Desk: 999 Canada Pl: 604 683 2000; open 8am–4pm daily; www.destinationvancouver.com

FlyOver™ Canada: 201-999 Canada Pl; 1-855 463 4822; open 9:30am–10pm daily; adm; www.flyovercanada.com

■ Underground paid parking is available here. Cheaper parking can be found at the north end of Burrard Street.

🔟⭐ Capilano Suspension Bridge Park

For thrill appeal, few sites rival Capilano Suspension Bridge Park. The park's star attraction is the marvelous suspension footbridge that sways 230 ft (70 m) above the gushing Capilano River. Visitors can also get a squirrel's-eye perspective of the West Coast rain forest that lies along treetop bridges or walk across a spectacular cliffside walkway straddling the deep Capilano Canyon. With a host of activities for both children and adults, this park is one of Vancouver's most popular attractions.

1 Suspension Bridge

This awe-inspiring bridge is built of steel cables spanning 450 ft (137 m) and strong enough to support a full Boeing 747. Those crossing the bridge **(right)** cling to the hand-rails as they experience the same thrills visitors did back in 1889.

2 The Kia'palano Big House

Set at the center of the Kia'palano Big House is the Next Generation story pole, honoring First Nations artists. An interactive exhibit with a Squamish Nation interpreter is in the Little Big House (a smaller version of the Big House).

3 Treetops Adventure

This exhilarating exhibit leads you gently upwards over seven suspension bridges attached to eight old-growth Douglas fir trees **(left)**. At the end of your journey, you are 100 ft (30 m) high in the mid-story treetops.

4 Treetops Technology

Treetops Adventure uses an innovative compression system to secure observation platforms to the trees. Instead of nails or screws, friction collars are used. Held on by compression, they exert a gentle pressure.

5 Cliffwalk

Almost 700 ft (213 m) of bridges **(above)** and stairs lead along the cliff edge, offering stunning views of the Capilano River gorge 230 ft (70 m) below.

6 Canyon Lights

From November to January, the suspension bridge and the Cliffwalk are illuminated with a changing display featuring thousands of multicolored lights, creating an impressive spectacle.

7 Totem Poles

At the Kia'palano entrance, totem poles **(right)** carved by local Coast Salish First Nations people make a colorful display. Introduced in the 1930s, the poles now number more than 30.

8 Locals from the Past

Friendly costumed guides in period attire welcome visitors to the park. Taking on the roles of local historical characters, the guides narrate the often hair-raising stories of the North Shore's past, when timber was king.

9 Living Forest

Clever interactive displays educate visitors about native plants and trees. Panels feature the animals and bugs living in a West Coast rain forest, and naturalists offer guided tours on its peaceful forest trails.

A LASTING LEGACY

Scotsman George Grant MacKay loved the outdoors. As Vancouver's first park commissioner, he voted for Stanley Park in 1886. Two years later, he bought 9 sq miles (23 sq km) of old-growth forest along the Capilano River and built a cabin on the edge of the canyon wall. With the help of local Coast Salish people, he built a hemp rope and cedar suspension bridge in 1889. This was the park's first bridge.

10 Story Centre

From miners to loggers to dancehall girls, the centre tells the history of the park, and of wider North Vancouver in a walk-through exhibit **(below)**. Many captioned photographs bring history to life. Voices from the Past, an audio component, fills in any blanks.

NEED TO KNOW

MAP B1 ■ 3735 Capilano Rd, North Vancouver ■ 604 985 7474 ■ www.capbridge.com

Open Hours vary, check website

Adm adults $66.95, seniors $61.95, students $53.95, youth (13–16) $36.95, children $26.95 (under-5s free)

■ There are two restaurants in the park serving West Coast classics while the various cafés on-site offer coffee as well as a range of snacks.

■ The free seasonal shuttle picks up park visitors from three downtown locations.

■ If heights are a concern when crossing the bridge, focus on the back of the person in front. It's worth making the trip across.

TOP 10 ★ Museum of Anthropology at UBC

Founded in 1947 and located in a breathtaking setting at the University of British Columbia (UBC), this museum houses one of the world's finest displays of First Nations, Métis, and Inuit art. Here you'll also find European ceramics, Asian textiles, Greek and Roman pottery, and African masks, as well as many full-size totem poles and contemporary carvings. The magnificent building, designed by Canadian architect Arthur Erickson, is a historic work of art inspired by the post-and-beam structures of Northwest Coast First Nations.

① Welcome Figure

On the museum's outdoor welcome plaza stands a red cedar welcome figure holding a *fisher* (an animal believed to have healing powers). It was created by Musqueam artist Susan Point.

③ Haida Houses

Two full-size Haida Houses **(above)** stand outside, surrounded by a forest of soaring, full-scale totem poles. They were designed in 1962 by contemporary Haida artist Bill Reid and Namgis artist Doug Cramer.

④ Totem Poles

Towering totem poles **(below)** from many First Nations are showcased beneath the glass walls of the Great Hall. The impressive structure of the hall provides a perfect setting for the poles.

② Bentwood Boxes

These boxes **(above)**, used for cooking as well as storage, are made in a very special way. The four sides are composed of one piece of cedar, which is steamed and bent to form the shape of the box before the base is added.

⑤ The Raven and the First Men

This massive sculpture **(right)**, by Bill Reid, is one of the most famous carvings in the world. It shows the figure of Raven (a wise yet mischievous trickster) discovering the first Haida humans and coaxing them out into the world from a giant clamshell.

GOING DEEP UNDERGROUND

The museum is built on three World War II gun emplacements, which were incorporated into the design of the building. Two are located outside the grounds, one of which is the platform for Bill Reid's *Raven*. A maze of secret tunnels connects the bunkers under the building.

⑦ Athenian Black Band Cup

Housed in the classical pottery collection, this cup was made in Greece in 540–530 BCE. It is attributed to the "Centaur Painter," one of a group of artists well-known for decorating drinking cups used in Athens at famous symposia or loud drinking parties.

⑧ Ceramic Stove

The centerpiece of the Koerner Ceramics Gallery is a stove from Central or Eastern Europe, around 1500–1600. Its lead-glazed tiles depict popular religious figures of the time.

⑨ Carved Doors

These massive doors were carved from red cedar in 1976 by Gitxsan artists from the 'Ksan Historical Village (see p42). They tell the story of the first people of the Skeena River region in British Columbia.

⑩ Weaving

Weaving has always been important for Salish people – woven objects from 4,500 years ago have been excavated on Musqueam traditional territory, where the museum is located.

Museum of Anthropology at UBC

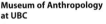
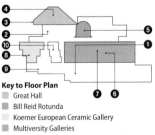

Key to Floor Plan

- Great Hall
- Bill Reid Rotunda
- Koerner European Ceramic Gallery
- Multiversity Galleries

⑥ New Guinea Necklaces

These ornate necklaces form part of the museum's founding collection of South Pacific materials, donated in 1927 by Canadian explorer Frank Burnett.

NEED TO KNOW

MAP A2 ▪ 6393 NW Marine Dr
▪ 604 822 5087 ▪ www.moa.ubc.ca

Open Hours vary, check website for more details

Adm adults $15, seniors & students $13, under-6s free, flat fee 5–9pm Thu $10

▪ The museum shop is renowned for its outstanding selection of original gold and silver jewelry, prints, argillite, textiles, and other treasures.

▪ Parking is available at the Rose Garden Parkade, opposite the museum.

▪ Koerner's Pub, across the street from the museum, is a good option for food and drinks.

🔟 ⭐ Vancouver Art Gallery

The Vancouver Art Gallery is the largest art gallery in Western Canada. Permanent collections include significant works of local landscape artists, the Group of Seven, plus works by BC artists such as Emily Carr and Bill Reid. The gallery specializes in impressive national and international exhibitions too, with innovative approaches to established artists as well as contemporary visionaries. The gallery has more than 11,000 works, including a large collection of photo-based art by Vancouver's international art superstar Jeff Wall and renowned Haida artist Robert Davidson. Housed in a Neo-Classical heritage building redesigned by acclaimed local architect Arthur Erickson, the gallery opened in 1983.

EMILY CARR

Although Emily Carr was born into a very wealthy Victoria family in 1871, the eccentric artist chose an alternative lifestyle instead, painting on a budget, often in the old-growth forests of Haida Gwaii. It was only in 1937 that the Vancouver Art Gallery bought one of her works. Largely overlooked during her lifetime, Carr's works now command some of the highest prices in Canada.

2 First Nations Art

Paintings, carvings, and sculpture by Indigenous artists are part of the gallery's rotating permanent collection, which includes sculptures by late Haida master carver Bill Reid. Reflecting the Modernist style of many First Nations artists, *Eagles* **(below)**, by Haida artist Robert Davidson, combines principles of abstraction with traditional First Nations iconography.

1 Court House Building

Built in 1912 as the Provincial Court House, the building reflects the imposing style of the era's leading Canadian architect, Francis Rattenbury.

3 Architecture

Architectural icon Arthur Erickson added 41,400 sq ft (3,715 sq m) of exhibition space to the old Provincial Court House when transforming it into the gallery's home **(below)**. Erickson retained many of the original features, including the courtroom, with its carved judge's bench.

4 Exhibitions Program

A celebration of Canadian female artists and the collective works of Yoko Ono and John Lennon are just a sample of the recent exhibitions shown at the VAG. Works of local and emerging talents from around the globe are also exhibited.

5 Art on the Rooftop

Vancouver artist Ken Lum's innovative *Four Boats Stranded: Red and Yellow, Black and White* stands out on the gallery's roof. The installation includes a scaled-down version of a First Nations longboat.

9 Jeff Wall Collection

Local artist Jeff Wall's photographic works, presented in large light boxes, focus on complex urban environments and feature images inspired by social issues.

10 Southern Façade

Overlooking Robson Street, the original steps into the court house are a popular meeting spot for locals. On the portico (below) is the work *Placed Upon the Horizon (Casting Shadows)* by Lawrence Weiner. Food trucks can be found at the plaza in front of the portico.

6 Emily Carr Collection

The Gallery holds more than 200 works by Emily Carr. This renowned West Coast artist studied local First Nations cultures, capturing their way of life in her paintings. Haida artifacts such as totem poles were a common subject. Stormy West Coast colors as seen, for example, in *Totem Poles, Kitseukla* (above), dominate her work. Items such as her tiny sketchbook are also on display.

NEED TO KNOW

MAP K3 ■ 750 Hornby St ■ 604 662 4700 ■ www.vanartgallery.bc.ca

Open 10am–5pm Sat–Wed (to 8pm Thu & Fri); closed Tue

Adm adult $29; under 18s free; entry free first Friday of the month 4–8pm

....

■ The 1931 Gallery Bistro patio is lovely on sunny days, and is ideal for catching a break in between exhibit tours. You do not need to pay admission to the gallery to eat at the bistro.

■ The Gallery Store sells contemporary art books, posters, paper goods, jewelry, and giftware, including a wide range of Emily Carr merchandise.

---

7 Photoconceptual Collection

The gallery is world-renowned for its permanent collection of contemporary photo-based art. It spans two decades and includes works by the Vancouver School of artists, such as Jeff Wall, Stan Douglas, Ian Wallace, and Ken Lum, as well as famous international artists Nancy Spero and Cindy Sherman, among others.

8 Family Programming

The gallery makes art accessible to younger visitors with family-focused activities every Sunday, as well as several "mega" family-oriented weekends each year. There are also regular events organized for teenagers.

Following pages Science World lit up at night

TOP 10 ⭐ Granville Island

Bustling Granville Island attracts millions of visitors every year, and rightly so. Where heavy industries once belched noxious fumes, street entertainers now amuse passersby with music, comedy, and magic. The Granville Island Public Market offers an enchanting mix of edibles and collectibles. More than 200 shops scattered throughout the Island sell everything from custom-made jewelry to yachts.

③ Net Loft

This intimate collection of boutiques sells unusual souvenirs, such as handmade paper, hats, offbeat postcards, beads of all kinds, and local and First Nations crafts.

④ Arts Club Theatre and Lounge

The Arts Club Theatre Company produces contemporary comedies and classics at the Granville Island Stage. The casual Backstage Lounge (see p88) showcases local bands.

① Kids Market

Fun is guaranteed in this fantasyland (above) for children. More than 20 shops sell everything from games and toys to pint-sized clothing.

② Marina and Maritime Market

Shops and services at the market include seafood merchants, tours, boat rentals, and marine souvenir shops. At the marina (below), yachts and sailboats are moored beside rustic fishing boats.

NEED TO KNOW

MAP H5 ■ www. granvilleisland.com

Kids Market and Net Loft: open 10am–6pm daily

Marina and Maritime Market: open 10am–6pm daily

Arts Club Theatre and Lounge: 1585 Johnston St; www.artsclub.com

Artisan Sake Maker: 1339 Railspur Alley; open 11:30am–6pm daily

Vancouver Studio Glass: 1440 Old Bridge St; open 11am–6pm Tue–Sun

Granville Island Public Market: open 9am–6pm daily; closed Mon in Jan

Granville Island Brewing: 1441 Cartwright St; open 11am–9pm daily

Craft Council of BC Shop & Gallery: 1386 Cartwright St; open 10am–5:30pm daily

7 Granville Island Public Market

The public market (see p86) is best known for its emporium of green grocers (left), butchers, bakers, fishmongers, importers, stalls selling multicultural foods, craft vendors, sweet stands, florists, and casual restaurants.

GRANVILLE ISLAND FERRIES

The Aquabus and False Creek Ferries fleets provide year-round services around False Creek, with sailings to and from downtown. They are a fun way to travel to Granville Island. Other routes include stops at Science World, Yaletown, and Vanier Park. Mini sunset cruises are also available.

5 Artisan Sake Maker

Award-winning local sake, made with fermented rice grown in the Fraser Valley of BC, can be sampled and purchased at this winery's store and tasting room. Delicious Japanese snacks accompany the tastings. Tours of the winery are also available.

8 Granville Island Brewing

Opened in 1984, this microbrewery (see p57) was the first of its kind in Canada. Their delicious beers (left) are made exclusively with natural ingredients. You can try these at one of the local pubs or in the brewery's on-site taproom after a behind-the-scenes tour and tasting session, offered daily.

10 Railspur District

The artisan studio-shops (below) in this laneway are run by painters, potters, and craftspeople who specialize in wood, fabric, leather, glass, and industrial cast-offs.

6 Vancouver Studio Glass

Watch local and national artists as they blow molten glass into beautiful vases, ornaments, jewelry, and dishes using traditional techniques. One of four furnaces keeps 150 lbs (70 kg) of glass molten at 2,000° F (1,100° C) around the clock.

9 Craft Council of BC Shop & Gallery

Exhibits here showcase fine art created by local artists in a range of mediums, including jewelery, ceramics, and wood carvings.

Granville Island

Brokers Bay

GRANVILLE BRIDGE

JOHNSTON ST

CARTWRIGHT ST

Sutcliffe Park

Alder Bay

TOP 10 ⭐ Science World

Fascinating insights into all aspects of the universe are featured at the award-winning Science World. Explorations begin with the smallest insect and progress to the farthest corners of the galaxy. A legacy of Expo '86, the building opened as a science center in 1989. Seven galleries feature hundreds of delightfully interactive, hands-on displays and exhibits based on different themes, as well as entertaining live science demonstrations.

1 Feature Exhibition

The best traveling exhibitions are showcased here. Always fresh and exciting, the content of the gallery is changed every few months. Consistently offering interactive opportunities for all ages to explore science topics including light, sound, engineering, and more, it's sure to spark your curiosity.

3 Geodesic Dome

Science World's 155-ft- (47-m-) tall geodesic dome **(above)** is dubbed "the golf ball" by locals. The design is based on the prototype structure made famous by US inventor and architect R. Buckminster Fuller. Mirror-like exterior panels, 766 in all, reflect the sunlight, while 391 exterior lights sparkle at night.

4 Living Lab

Living Lab offers a hands-on opportunity to participate in scientific research. It helps kids assess their cognitive development through fun activities.

5 Science Theatre

High-definition films on science, nature, and outer space are screened here. There are cartoons for toddlers as well as movies for the whole family.

Wonder Gallery 2

Designed for kids up to 5 years old, this area has a baby gym, water tables meant for splashing around, a climbing tower, a building blocks zone, and a bus laboratory for fun experiments **(right)**.

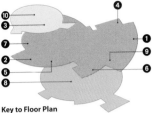

Key to Floor Plan
- Level 1
- Level 2
- Level 3

Science World

8 Peter Brown Family Centre Stage

Scientific principles and phenomena are explored in five daily shows. Presenters mix balloons and electricity, bubbles and fire to dazzle and captivate.

9 BodyWorks Gallery

This gallery encourages positive curiosity regarding the human body. Questions about how human beings hear, smell, and move are answered in this fun-filled interactive space.

Eureka! Gallery 7

Eureka! Gallery **(right)** explores universal themes such as water, air, motion and invention. Children and adults alike are invited to make their own discoveries in a lifelike science laboratory environment. You can even use an infrared camera to discover the hot spots on your body.

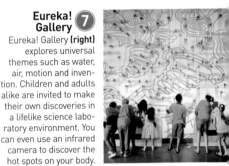

Search: Sara Stern Gallery 6

Explore natural history with live critters and creepy-crawlies, a replica of a beaver home, a real bee colony, and a life-size Tyrannosaurus rex skeleton cast **(right)** at this interactive gallery.

10 OMNIMAX® Theatre

The five-story screen, one of the largest in the world, envelops viewers with thrilling films. The 400-seat theater, located inside the dome, projects images nine times larger than a conventional movie house onto a screen that is 88 ft (27 m) in diameter.

NEED TO KNOW

MAP M5 ▪ 1455 Quebec St; 604 443 7440; www.scienceworld.ca

Open 10am–5pm daily (July–Aug: to 8pm, with half-price entry 5–8pm); closed Dec 25

Adm adults $33.20, seniors and youth (13–18) $26.75, children $22.50, under-2s free; additional fee for OMNIMAX® Theatre

▪ Triple O's, the fast food arm of popular BC burger chain, White Spot, is on the Science World site. A concession on Level 2 offers juices and ice-cream bars.

▪ Paid parking in the small lot is at a premium. Try taking the SkyTrain to Main Street Station, then walking to Science World.

▪ Meet the backyard chickens in the fascinating Ken Spencer Science Park located right outside the main center. A diverse range of crops and plants are grown in raised beds here, and visitors can learn a lot about environmental sustainability and recycling through interactive presentations. This part of Science World is open from March to October.

TOP 10 ⭐ Victoria

Picturesque Victoria is the perfect getaway from bustling Vancouver. Established as a fort in 1843 by the Hudson's Bay Company, Victoria became British Columbia (BC)'s capital in 1868, and the growing city attracted top architects such as Francis Mawson Rattenbury. Today the "Garden City" buzzes around the Inner Harbour, and nearby are some excellent museums, the oldest Chinatown in Canada, and the home of Victoria's most famous artist, Emily Carr.

GOVERNOR JAMES DOUGLAS

James Douglas, known as the father of British Columbia, was born in British Guiana (now called Guyana) in 1803. Working for the Hudson's Bay Company, Douglas established Fort Victoria in 1843 and set about turning it into a center of political power. Sir James Douglas was knighted before he died aged 74.

1 Royal BC Museum

This museum is known for its First Nations artifacts and art, as well as a fascinating collection of highlights from BC's history and its natural wonders *(see pp30–31)*. Changing exhibitions are highly thought-provoking. There are several totem poles outside.

2 Fairmont Empress Hotel

This luxury château-style hotel *(see p119)* was built by the Canadian Pacific Railway in 1908. The afternoon tea, served here daily, is a fine treat and an elegant experience.

4 Inner Harbour

The Inner Harbour **(above)** is the historic center of Victoria. A mix of yachts, fishing boats, ferries, and float planes dock here, while pedestrians happily stroll along a wide, curved walkway.

3 British Columbia Parliament Buildings

Impressive gray granite buildings house the provincial legislature. Overlooking the Inner Harbour, the Neo-Classical structure **(below)** is a wonderful sight at night, illuminated by 3,560 sparkling light bulbs.

5 Craigdarroch Castle

This four-story, 39-room stone mansion was built in the late 1880s for coal baron Robert Dunsmuir. Highlights include period furnishings, stained-glass windows **(above)**, and a grand oak staircase.

6 Beacon Hill Park

Noted for its gnarled Garry oak trees and 350-year-old Chinese bell, this park, dating from the mid-1800s, is a lovely place to stroll around and have a picnic.

7 Maritime Museum of British Columbia

This museum showcases BC's rich seafaring past, with 35,000 artifacts as well as informative walking tours of the Inner Harbour. Visitors can also learn about pirates and infamous shipwrecks, or try their hands at sailor's knot.

8 Emily Carr House

Built in 1864, the house that artist Emily Carr *(see p20)* was born in typifies the sensibilities of the Victorian era. The building has been described as both English Gingerbread as well as San Francisco Victorian, inspiring the restoration of many of the area's old houses.

9 Art Gallery of Greater Victoria

Housed in an 1889 mansion, this gallery is known for its Asian collection, including a Shinto shrine in the Asian garden. Paintings and literary work by local artist Emily Carr **(right)** are also featured.

10 Chinatown

The Chinatown in Victoria once rivaled San Francisco's for size. Today, the bustling two-block area is home to artists' studios, restaurants, and a wide range of shops.

NEED TO KNOW

Royal BC Museum: MAP P4; 675 Belleville St; 1 888 447 7977; open 10am–6pm daily; closed Jan 1 & Dec 25; adm; www.royalbcmuseum.bc.ca

Inner Harbour: MAP N3

British Columbia Parliament Buildings: MAP P4; 501 Belleville St; 250 387 3046; open for guided tours 8:30am–4:30pm daily; www.leg.bc.ca

Craigdarroch Castle: MAP E6; 1050 Joan Cres; 250 592 5323; open 10am–4pm Wed–Sun; closed 25, 26 Dec and 1 Jan; adm; www.thecastle.ca

Beacon Hill Park: MAP Q6; 250 385 5711; www.victoria.ca

Chinatown: MAP P1; Fisgard & Herald Sts at Government St

Maritime Museum of British Columbia: MAP P3; 744 Douglas St; 250 385 4222; open 10am–5pm Tue–Sat; adm; www.mmbc.bc.ca

Emily Carr House: MAP P6; 207 Government St; 250 383 5843; open 10am–3pm Tue–Sun; adm by donation; www.carrhouse.ca

Art Gallery of Greater Victoria: MAP E6; 1040 Moss St; 250 384 4171; open 10am–5pm Tue–Sat (to 9pm Thu), noon–5pm Sun; adm; www.aggv.ca

■ BC Ferries connects Vancouver with Victoria. BC Transit operates a large network of buses across the city *(see pp110–11)*.

■ A trip with Harbour Ferry *(250 514 9794; www.victoriaharbourferry.com)* is a great way to sight-see.

Royal BC Museum

1 BC Archives on Display

Learn about British Columbia directly from the provincial archives. The exhibition focuses on stories of notable characters and highlights prominent moments in the area's history.

2 Old Town, New Approach

Dedicated to cultural diversity, this exhibit works with community groups to share oft-overlooked aspects of the province's history, with a focus on Black, Asian, and Indigenous stories. Walk through townscapes of the past, visit old theaters and historical homes, and see a recreation of early Chinatown along the way.

3 Netherlands Centennial Carillon Tower

This tower, with 62 bells, was gifted to the museum in 1967 from BC residents of Dutch descent. Recitals are usually held at 3pm on Sundays in the summer.

First Nations totem pole

Netherlands Centennial Carillon Tower

4 Thunderbird Park

A dozen poles preside over this park. The carved mythical figures tell stories of traditional Coast Salish cultures. Included are Gitxsan memorial poles, Haida mortuary poles, a Cumshewa pole, and Kwakwaka'wakw heraldic poles.

5 Ocean Station

A Victorian-era "submarine" exhibit allows visitors to access BC's coastal marine life. Peer through portholes at kelp beds, watch live sea creatures, including sea urchins and fish, in the central 95-gallon (360-liter) aquarium, then check out the colorful vistas on a giant underwater cliff through a moveable periscope.

6 St. Ann's Schoolhouse

Built in 1844 and donated to the museum by the Sisters of St. Ann, this building was once a school classroom. It was moved to its current location in 1974 and is now an interpretive center.

7 Mungo Martin House

Also called Wawadit'la, this replica of a big house was built in 1952 by Chief Mungo Martin, who was considered the finest carver of his day, with the assistance of his family. The house posts bear the family's crest. Wawadit'la is a functioning big house and is still used for First Nations events with the permission of Chief Martin's grandson.

8 IMAX Victoria Theatre

Subjects as diverse as whales and outer space are explored in a series of documentary and feature films on the theater's six-story screen.

9 Natural History Gallery

Realistic dioramas explore a range of environments, from ocean to boreal forest, including the giant old-growth forest that once covered coastal BC. One of the most striking of the range of animals depicted in re-created habitats is a grizzly bear, BC's largest land predator. Other highlights include full-size models of a woolly mammoth and a northern (or Steller) sea lion.

Exterior of the Helmcken House

10 Helmcken House

One of the oldest houses in BC still on its original site was built by Dr. John Sebastian Helmcken in 1852. The three-room log structure is made of Douglas fir trees. Period furnishings reflect the Victorian era.

RECONCILIATION AND REPATRIATION

In March 2017, The Royal BC Museum organized a symposium in partnership with the First Peoples' Cultural Council. This gathering in Kelowna, BC, was to discuss the repatriation of Indigenous ancestral remains, sacred objects and cultural heritage items in the museum's collection. Public attention has been focused on reconciliation with BC's First Nations since the Truth and Reconciliation Commission (TRC) of Canada revealed the harm done to the more than 150,000 First Nations, Métis, and Inuit children removed from their communities and forced to attend residential schools *(see p39)*. The TRC report reinforced the rights of Indigenous peoples to restitution of their heritage, including many items now exhibited in museums across North America and Europe. The museum's First Peoples Gallery is under renovation.

TOP 10 MUSEUM OBJECTS

1 Dinosaur footprints Cast from imprints in Peace River Canyon.

2 Woolly Mammoth This model is in the Natural History gallery.

3 Indigenous canoes These historic modes of transportation are culturally significant.

4 Huu-ay-aht welcome figures Pre-1900 carved figures are exhibited in the lobby.

5 Elza Mayhew sculpture Mayhew's imposing totemic bronze "Caryatid."

6 Captain Cook dagger The weapon that was used to kill the explorer.

7 Judge Begbie's wig This was worn by BC's first supreme court judge.

8 Cougar BC's largest wild cat is in the Coastal Forest diorama.

9 Haida box by Bill Reid Bill Reid made this gold box in 1971.

10 Chinese tailoring shop A reassembled shop in the Old Town.

Hereditary chiefs gather along with friends and family to witness the historical repatriation of the nuxalk totem pole carved by the late Louie Snow.

TOP 10 ★ Around Tofino

Vancouver Island's west coast around Tofino offers pristine wilderness, old-growth rain forest, endless beaches, and mystical vistas. Bald eagles appear in large numbers in Clayoquot Sound, a UNESCO biosphere reserve, while the Pacific Ocean teems with Dall's porpoises, sea lions, and seals. Surfing, fishing, kayaking, hiking, and storm watching are superb.

1 Long Beach

Rolling waves thrash the sandy shores of this seemingly endless beach, 15.5 miles (25 km) in length. Temperate rain forests featuring giant Sitka spruce and cedars border the beach. The Pacific Ocean rollers offer year-round surfing.

2 Roy Henry Vickers Gallery

The cedar-planked gallery in Tofino is a tranquil hand-hewn longhouse traditional to the local First Nations people. Internationally acclaimed Tsimshian printmaker Roy Henry Vickers is the gallerist.

Around Tofino

[map showing locations around Tofino: Clayoquot Sound, Vancouver Island Range, Kakawis, Tofino Inlet, Tofino, Kennedy Lake, Kildonan, Ucluelet, Broken Group Islands, Tzartus Island, Sarita, Bamfield]

GRAY WHALES

Each year, an estimated 20,000 gray whales migrate past the Vancouver Island coast around Long Beach. They are on an 11,000-mile (17,700-km) round trip, migrating south from the Arctic to their breeding grounds off southern California and Mexico between the months of December and early February, and returning north from March through May.

3 Ucluelet

This small town **(below)** is the gateway to multiple outdoor activities on both land and water. Avid fishers flock here for steelhead, sturgeon, halibut, and Pacific and freshwater salmon. The climate is temperate, with 328 frost-free days a year.

Kwisitis Visitor Centre 4
Displays at this center (right) show the natural history of the area and introduce historic cultural objects of the local Nuu-chah-nulth people.

5 Wild Pacific Trail
This 10-mile (16-km) trail runs alongside the ocean through rain forest, from the tip of the Ucluelet peninsula to the Pacific Rim National Park.

9 Tofino
This pretty coastal town was named by the Spanish explorer Juan Francisco de la Bodega y Quadra after one of his teachers, a hydrographer. Located at the entrance to Clayoquot Sound (see p92), and with just 1,900 residents, Tofino provides easy access to idyllic beaches, and is a magnet for outdoor adventurers, winter storm watchers, and foodies.

6 Meares Island
Accessed by boat or water taxi, visitors to Meares Island (above) can walk the Boardwalk Trail to the hanging garden tree, an ancient red cedar.

7 Pacific Rim National Park Reserve
This park is a famous spot for whale-watching, and spans three distinct areas: Long Beach, the West Coast Trail, and the Broken Group Islands.

8 West Coast Trail
The West Coast Trail is a challenging 46-mile (75-km) hike along a historic path built to help shipwrecked mariners. Waterfalls, arches, and caves dot the rocky coast.

NEED TO KNOW

Long Beach: MAP A4

Roy Henry Vickers Gallery: MAP A4; 350 Campbell St, Tofino; open 10am–5pm daily; www.roy henryvickers.com

Ucluelet: MAP B5; www. discoverucluelet.com

Kwisitis Visitor Centre: MAP B5; 485 Wick Rd,

Ucluelet; www.go tofino.com

Wild Pacific Trail: www. wildpacifictrail.com

Meares Island: MAP A4

Pacific Rim National Park Reserve: www.pc.gc.ca

West Coast Trail: www.pc.gc.ca

Tofino: MAP A4; www. tourismtofino.com

Hot Springs Cove: MAP A4; arrange in advance

10 Hot Springs Cove
A popular outing 23 miles (37 km) to the northwest of Tofino is Hot Springs Cove (above), reached by floatplane or boat. Stroll on a boardwalk through old-growth rain forest, before immersing yourself in one of the rocky geothermal pools.

TOP 10 ★ Whistler

The 75-mile (120-km) drive to Whistler from Vancouver showcases stunning scenery, a combination of Howe Sound's sparkling blue waters and the majestic snow-covered Coast Mountain range. The magnificent side-by-side peaks of Whistler and Blackcomb mountains welcome more than two million visitors every year. A year-round resort, Whistler has hosted both the Olympic and the Paralympic Winter Games. While the resort is known for its hotels, restaurants, and shops, it still preserves five lakes and beautiful natural enclaves of forests.

1 Blackcomb Mountain

Nicknamed the "Mile High Mountain," Blackcomb towers over Whistler resort at an elevation of 7,992 ft (2,436 m). Skiers can choose from more than 100 marked runs. In summer, Horstman Glacier is unmissable.

3 Whistler Mountain

Skiers and snowboarders can enjoy 7.4 sq miles (19.3 sq km) of thrilling terrain with more than 100 marked trails (right). Whistler Village Gondola offers superb views of Whistler Valley during the 20-minute ride to the top. Mountain biking and alpine hiking are great summer activities.

4 Whistler Village

This pedestrian-only Alpine-style enclave, ringed by shops, hotels, and restaurants, provides ski-in, ski-out access to Whistler Mountain. It's busy round the clock.

2 Fairmont Chateau Whistler

Whistler's grand dame (above) reigns over the valley from the Upper Village. The antique furnishings, gold-leaf ceiling, and Canadian art in the lobby of this chateau-style hotel make it well worth a visit. The opulent Mallard Lounge has a popular heated patio.

NEED TO KNOW

MAP F1

Whistler Visitor Centre: 4230 Gateway Dr; 604 935 3357; www.whistler.com

Fairmont Chateau Whistler: 4599 Chateau Blvd; 604 938 8000; www.fairmont.com

■ Take waterproof and warm clothes up the mountains, even in the summer.

■ Horstman Hut is the highest restaurant here, sitting at 7,494 ft (2,284 m).

■ A free shuttle every 15 to 20 minutes connects hotels and condos to ski slopes. BC Transit buses take guests to and from the villages and town. You can also call Whistler Taxi (604 932 3333) or use the app.

■ Ride PEAK 2 PEAK from Whistler to Blackcomb mountains on one of the world's highest gondolas.

6 Valley Trail

The lovely 25-mile (40-km) Valley Trail **(left)** attracts walkers, cyclists, and in-line skaters. It leads past Lost Lake, Rainbow Park, and Alta, Nita, and Alpha lakes, through stands of trees that fringe residential areas. In winter, the Lost Lake loop is dedicated to cross-country skiing.

BEAR SAFETY

Watch out for black bears on the Valley Trail, especially in the early morning or evening. Be sure to observe rules: don't approach or feed them, don't run, and stay calm. On hikes, make noise, wear bear bells, carry bear spray, and keep dogs on a leash.

8 Upper Village

Nestled at the base of Blackcomb Mountain, the Upper Village offers easy access to the slopes. The ski-in, ski-out luxury hotels, restaurants, and shops are unsurpassed. In summer, Adventure Zone is great for kids.

9 Village North

Construction of Village North followed that of Upper Village, with the added attractions of vehicle access, a shopping mall, cafés, restaurants, and lifestyle shops.

Whistler

5 Alta Lake

This area was once home to Rainbow Lodge, Whistler's first resort. Traces of it remain at Rainbow Park **(below)**. Explore the lake's perimeter on the paved Valley. You can hike, swim, wind surf, or canoe here.

7 Creekside

An investment of several million dollars has transformed this activity center, providing chic hotels and a mini-mall. Skiers can access Whistler Mountain from this historic base at the Creekside Gondola.

10 Green Lake

A glacial gem with crystal-clear water thanks to mountain melt, Green Lake is spectacularly situated between some of the area's highest peaks, including massive Mount Currie.

The Top 10 of Everything

Visitors walking the Cliffwalk at
Capilano Suspension Bridge Park

Moments in History

① First Nations Traditional Territory

The city now called Vancouver has been the traditional, ancestral homeland of the Coast Salish peoples, specifically the Musqueam, Squamish, and Tsleil-Waututh Nations since time immemorial. Vancouver Island is the traditional land of the Coast Salish, Nuu-chah-nulth, and Kwakwaka'wakw peoples, with Victoria home to the Lekwungen people (Esquimalt and Songhees Nations).

Illustration of Hudson's Bay Company

② 1790s: Arrival of the Europeans

Captain James Cook landed on the west coast of Vancouver Island in 1778, but both the island and the future city were to be named after British Captain George Vancouver, who explored Burrard Inlet in 1792. He visited only briefly, as at that time the Spanish had laid claim to the territory. European arrival and eventual settlement would prove devastating to Indigenous people.

③ 1808: Simon Fraser Mistakes the Columbia River

In 1808 Simon Fraser set out to try to find a direct route for the fur trade to the Pacific. He followed what he thought was the Columbia River but, after a perilous expedition, he realized the river he had found emptied into the Strait of Georgia, so it couldn't possibly be the Columbia. The mouth of the Fraser River (as it became known) is the site of present-day Vancouver.

④ 1821: Hudson's Bay Company

At the beginning of the 19th century, Canada experienced competition in the fur trade between the North West Company and the Hudson's Bay Company. In 1821 the two merged, and in 1828 Hudson's Bay set up trading outpost Fort Yale on the Fraser River.

⑤ 1850s: Gold Fever

After gold was found in the Fraser River, Fort Yale underwent a population explosion. Rapid economic expansion in the region led to the area being declared a British Crown Colony.

⑥ 1868: Victoria becomes the Capital City

Fort Victoria formed the central hub of the fledgling province of British Columbia. During the Gold Rush, all miners were expected to report there before receiving a license, and the city quickly became a major seaport and trading center. In 1868 the city was named British Columbia's capital.

⑦ 1887: Canadian Pacific Terminus

A huge turning point in the fortunes of Vancouver was the decision to relocate the terminus of the Canadian Pacific Railway from Port Moody. The terminus was moved 14 miles (22 km) east to what was then called Granville (quickly renamed to Vancouver). The first train pulled in on May 23, 1887.

8 1908: The University of British Columbia is Established

In 1899, Vancouver College was established, affiliated with Montreal's McGill University, and in 1908 the first steps toward an independent university *(see p103)* were taken. Point Grey was the designated spot, but it took 17 years before its inauguration.

9 2010: Winter Olympics and Paralympics

A joint bid between Vancouver and Whistler *(see pp34–5)*, the Winter Games were based at the BC Place Stadium and cost close to $2 billion. As part of investment for the Games, the Sea-to-Sky highway was improved, the Canada Line transit to Richmond opened, and the Olympic Village was built.

10 2021: Unmarked Graves

From the 1860s to the 1980s, mandatory residential boarding schools had been established all over the country with the aim of assimilating First Nations, Inuit, and Métis children into Canadian society. The students were denied their traditional languages, religion, family, and way of life. In 2021, hundreds of unmarked graves of Indigenous children were discovered at the grounds of these schools across British Columbia. Searches are underway for other unmarked graves as a result.

Memorial for the Indigenous children

TOP 10 FAMOUS VANCOUVERITES

The inspirational Dr. David Suzuki

1 Dr. David Suzuki
A contemporary scientist, broadcaster, and environmentalist, Suzuki inspires individuals to protect the natural world.

2 Pauline Johnson
Credited for naming Stanley Park's Lost Lagoon, Johnson (1861–1913) published First Nations legends and lore in English.

3 Joseph Seraphim Fortes
Joe came to Vancouver from Trinidad, via England, in 1885. As Vancouver's first lifeguard, he saved hundreds of lives.

4 Emily Carr
From Victoria rather than Vancouver, Carr's Modernist and landscape art features prominently in the Vancouver Art Gallery *(see pp20–21)*.

5 Chief Joe Capilano
Sa7plek (Sahp-luk) or Kiyapalanexw (anglicized to Capilano) sought greater rights for Indigenous peoples.

6 Michael J. Fox
A Hollywood A-list actor, Fox was diagnosed with Parkinson's disease in the 1990s and set up a non-profit foundation for Parkinson's research.

7 Douglas Coupland
Known for his 1991 novel *Generation X*, Coupland grew up in West Vancouver.

8 Michael Bublé
The singer and songwriter started out in a downtown club on Granville Street.

9 Seth Rogen
Aged just 16, Rogen and his family headed from Vancouver to LA to launch his career as an actor and producer.

10 Heather Ogden
Before becoming Principal Dancer at the National Ballet of Canada in 2005, Heather Ogden trained at the Richmond Academy of Dance.

TOP10 Museums and Art Galleries

Wood Interior by Emily Carr

1 Vancouver Art Gallery

The gallery's collection *(see pp20–21)* is rich in historic and contemporary works by both BC and international artists, including the world's largest collection of Emily Carr pieces. The splendid *fin de siècle* exhibition hall hosts exhibits.

2 Chinese Canadian Museum

MAP M4 ■ 51 E Pender St ■ 604 658 8880 ■ Open 10am–5pm Wed–Sun ■ Adm ■ www.chinesecanadian museum.ca

This modern museum celebrates Chinese Canadian history. The museum is housed in the Wing Sang Building, the oldest structure in Chinatown.

3 Roedde House Museum

MAP J3 ■ 1415 Barclay St ■ 604 684 7040 ■ Open 1–4pm Wed–Fri & Sun (Jun–Aug: from 11am) ■ Adm ■ www.roeddehouse.org

This is the only museum in the city set in a heritage house, with original 19th-century architecture and beautifully restored artifacts. It regularly hosts small, intimate concerts.

4 BC Sports Hall of Fame and Museum

BC's sports achievements, including those of local heroes Terry Fox and his Marathon of Hope *(see 76)* and Rick Hansen's Man in Motion World Tour, are celebrated in this gallery space *(see p77)*. The Participation Gallery here entices visitors to try out pitching, sprinting, and rock climbing.

5 Inuit Gallery

MAP L3 ■ 120 Carrie Cates Ct ■ 604 688 7323 ■ Open 10am–6pm Mon–Sat, 11am–5pm Sun ■ www.inuit.com

One of the region's most respected commercial galleries, the Inuit Gallery shows an outstanding, museum-quality selection of Inuit and Northwest Coast First Nations sculpture, graphics, and jewelry.

6 Museum of Vancouver

Permanent and short-term exhibits *(see p85)* offer an intimate look at Vancouver's heritage. The hands-on exhibits, such as the 1950s

Futuristic exterior of the Museum of Vancouver

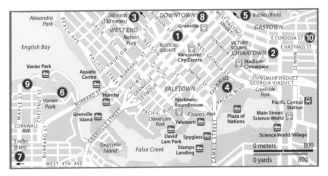

soda shop and the interactive depiction of the 1960s hippie era, make history a delight.

⑦ Museum of Anthropology at UBC

Situated on cliffs overlooking Burrard Inlet, this museum *(see pp18–19)* focuses primarily on the coastal First Nations and aims at bringing Indigenous art into the mainstream. The museum's galleries house over 500,000 ethnographic and archaeological objects from around the world.

Exhibit in the Museum of Anthropology at UBC

⑧ Bill Reid Gallery

One of Canada's greatest artists, Bill Reid (1920–98) helped introduce the Northwest Coast's Indigenous art traditions to a wider audience through his work. This gallery *(see p77)* has over 60 pieces of his jewelry, and works by contemporary Inuit and First Nations artists.

⑨ Vancouver Maritime Museum

Exhibits of artifacts, models, vessels, and photos pay tribute to Canada's marine heritage *(see p84)*. At the heart of the collection is the restored 104-ft (32-m) schooner *St. Roch*, the second ship to navigate the North West Passage, but the first to travel it from west to east.

⑩ Vancouver Police Museum

Enter the old city morgue, which now serves as the police museum's forensic laboratory, and it's not difficult to imagine the coroner leaning over the slab, about to start an examination. The 20,000 artifacts housed here offer an intriguing glimpse into the dark world of crime and punishment in Vancouver's past *(see p69)*. Exhibits include confiscated weapons, counterfeit bills, and displays showing scientific evidence. You may find yourself amid a gaggle of wide-eyed children, as school tours play an important part in the programming.

Exhibits at Vancouver Police Museum

🔟 Indigenous Art

Bronze sculpture *The Jade Canoe* by Haida sculptor Bill Reid

1 The Jade Canoe
MAP A2 ▪ Vancouver International Airport

Haida artist Bill Reid's awe-inspiring bronze creation is the second casting of *The Black Canoe*. Thirteen characters from Haida mythology paddle an imposing 20-ft (6-m) canoe.

2 Carved Doors
The entrance to the Museum of Anthropology at UBC *(see p19)* is itself a work of art. Made of red cedar by four Gitxsan master carvers, the double doors convey a narrative from the Skeena River region. When closed, these images form the shape of a Northwest Coast bentwood box, objects used by First Nations people for storage and burials.

3 Hetux
MAP A2
▪ Vancouver International Airport

Travelers at Vancouver airport are greeted by *Hetux*, a huge birch-and-aluminum sculpture. Connie Watts here combined the form of the mythical thunderbird with features of wolves, wrens salmon, and hummingbirds to reflect the untamed spirit of her grandmother.

4 Chief of the Undersea World
Orcas were still kept at the Vancouver Aquarium *(see p13)* when Haida artist Bill Reid's sculpture was installed outside it in 1984. The 16-ft- (5-m-) tall bronze killer whale leaping into the air remains as a tribute to this native West Coast creature.

5 Thunderbird House Post
A majestic thunderbird stands atop a grizzly bear, which is depicted holding a human being. The house post is a replica of one of a pair carved in the early 1900s by artist Charlie James. After 40 years in Stanley Park, the deteriorated poles were restored and moved indoors. Carver Tony Hunt re-created the post now in the park's Brockton Point Visitor Centre *(see p13)*.

6 'Ksan Mural
MAP K3
▪ 1025 W Georgia St (inside RBC Royal Bank)

Five artists carved this red cedar frieze showing Northwest Coast raven myths. The nine panels tell stories of how the Raven created the elements of the world through his mischievous activities.

Thunderbird House Post

7 One of the World's Tallest Totem Poles
MAP Q6
Raised in Beacon Hill Park *(see p29)* in 1956, the pole, by Kwakwaka'wakw chief Mungo Martin with David Martin and Henry Hunt, took six months to carve from a 128-ft- (39-m-) tall cedar.

8 Kwakwaka'wakw Heraldic Pole
This pole, at Victoria's Royal BC Museum *(see pp30–31)*, is at the museum's Thunderbird Longhouse. It was originally carved in 1952–53 by Mungo Martin and his family and has since been restored by his great-grandson among others. It's stood at this spot for over 70 years.

9 Coast Salish Welcome Figures
MAP A2 ▪ Vancouver International Airport
Two 17-ft- (5-m-) tall red cedar figures welcome airport arrivals in traditional Musqueam style. Musqueam Coast Salish artist Susan Point carved both from the same log.

Inukshuk sculpture by Alvin Kanak

10 Inukshuk
MAP G3 ▪ English Bay Beach
Made by Alvin Kanak for Expo '86, this granite sculpture is an Inuit welcome figure, a traditional traveler's marker, although much larger than those found in the Arctic.

TOP 10 PUBLIC ARTWORKS

A-maze-ing Laughter, Morton Park

1 A-maze-ing Laughter
MAP G3 & H4 ▪ Denman and Davie Sts
Crowds tend to gather around these playful figures in Morton Park.

2 Photo Session
MAP B2 ▪ Queen Elizabeth Park
Join Seward Johnson's family of bronze figures posing for a snapshot.

3 The Crab
MAP G4 ▪ 1100 Chestnut St
Admire George Norris's stylized stainless-steel sculpture of a crab.

4 Gate to the Pacific Northwest
MAP G4 ▪ Vanier Park
Alan Chung Hung's sculpture invokes 18th-century navigation instruments.

5 Douglas Coupland's Digital Orca
MAP K2 ▪ Vancouver Convention and Exhibition Centre
This piece captures the spirit of Vancouver's harborfront.

6 Salute to the Lions of Vancouver
MAP L2 ▪ 999 Canada Pl
Gathie Falk's steel lions align with Lions Gate Bridge and The Lions mountain.

7 Angel of Victory
MAP L3 ▪ 601 W Cordova St
Coeur de Lion MacCarthy's bronze angel lifts a World War I soldier heavenward.

8 Street Light
MAP K5 ▪ Marinaside Cres
Panels showing images of historic events cast shadows onto a walkway.

9 Pendulum
MAP K3 ▪ 885 W Georgia St
This stunning seven-story kinetic sculpture is by Alan Storey.

10 Should I Be Worried?
MAP L5 ▪ False Creek
This neon sign by Justin Langlois aims at initiating dialogue on sustainability.

🔟 Off the Beaten Track

Granville street in downtown Vancouver

1 Vancouver Underground

MAP M4 ■ 251 E Georgia St.

Those looking for nightlife beyond Granville Street strip can dip into one of the city's secret speakeasies or underground clubs. Order the "number 7" at Blnd Tger Dumplings to enter Laowai, a swanky, hidden lounge inspired by prohibition-era China. Alternatively, visit Guilt & Co (p72), an underground music venue that hosts live performances every night.

2 Asian Eats

From sushi to dim sum, Vancouver's Asian food scene is thriving, thanks to a large and diverse diaspora population. For acclaimed gourmet delights and tasting menus, head to either Miku (p58) or Bao Bei (p73). If you're in the mood for something more casual, the city's numerous street food joints have much to offer.

3 Hidden Hikes

Tower Beach: MAP A2 ■ Mount Strachan: MAP E3; 6000 Cypress Bowl Rd

Take a step back in time by hiking on these two lesser-known trails. In Vancouver, head to Tower Beach via Pacific Spirit Park Trails 3 or 4 to see two graffiti-covered searchlight towers used by the Canadian military against Japanese submarines in World War II. On the North Shore, ascend scenic Mount Strachan where remnants of a Royal Canadian Navy jet crash can still be seen.

4 Breweries

When it comes to Vancouver's local craft beer scene, Mount Pleasant (p61) is the place to be. This buzzy neighborhood marks the heart of the city's ale trail, with a flurry of breweries offering plenty of opportunities for a beer crawl. Elsewhere, west coast hops are served up in city favorites such as Yaletown Brewing (p88) and Granville Island Brewing (p88).

Cycling along Stanley Park's biking trail

5 Street Art
MAP H5 ■ Granville Island
■ https://granvilleisland.com/news/outdoor-mural-gallery-open

Granville Island (p24) is popular for its market, but there's also an easy-to-miss lovely outdoor mural gallery, known as the Chain & Forge. Covering two former parking lots, the gallery features Indigenous art by local Musqueam artist Debra Sparrow and the loud, punchy colours of South Asian-Canadian artist Sandeep Johal.

6 Bike Routes
Ontario St: MAP M5 & M6; Adanac Bike Route: MAP M4

Known as a cycle-friendly city, Vancouver is worth seeing by bike. The city has much more to offer than the iconic Stanley Park seawall. Heading south, ride up the Ontario Street hill until you reach the lush Queen Elizabeth Park (p104) or pedal into East Van along the quaint and well-traveled Adanac bike route (which is Canada spelled backwards).

7 Hogan's Alley
MAP M4 ■ www.hogans alleysociety.org

Hogan's Alley was the former home of Vancouver's Black community in what's now known as the Strathcona neighborhood. Before the community was displaced due to construction of the Dunsmuir and Georgia viaducts in 1971, famous musician Jimi Hendrix's grandmother, Nora Hendrix, was one of its best-known residents. She founded the city's first Black church, which still stands today.

8 Lesser-known Galleries
Polygon Gallery: 101 Carrie Cates Ct ■ https://thepolygon.ca

On a rainy day, go on a free, self-guided art tour through the city's under-the-radar galleries. Chinatown's Skwachàys Lodge (p117) is one of the best. This boutique hotel also offers housing and studio workspaces to local Indigenous artists.

The inspiring Polygon Gallery in North Shore, Vancouver

North Shore's Polygon Gallery is another highlight; photography and media-based art are at the forefront here (admission is by donation).

9 Hip Neighborhoods
Mount Pleasant: MAP M6

Known for breweries, vintage shops, trendy cafés, mom and pop grocers, and streetside patios, Mount Pleasant (p61) and Commercial Drive (p60) are some of the city's coolest places off the standard tourist track. Though both neighborhoods are gentrifying, their working-class, counterculture roots still shine through. Experience the coffee culture on Commercial, and duck into Mount Pleasant's alleys to admire walls painted for the Vancouver Mural Festival.

10 Parks
MAP L5 ■ 1616 Columbia St
■ https://covapp.vancouver.ca

With such a mild climate, parks are the year-round gathering place for Vancouverites and every neighborhood has its favorite. For a great spot to take in the seaside cityscape, try Habitat Island, accessed by a sandspit off the seawall in the False Creek neighborhoods (p85). Further afield in Burnaby, Deer Park Lake (p104) promises gorgeous lake views and winding trails.

🔟 Beaches and Bays

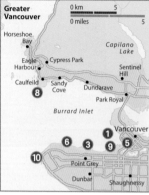

1 English Bay

This beautiful bay is a popular West End attraction. On New Year's Day it hosts the Polar Bear Swim, when thousands of swimmers brave the cold waters. A more popular year-round activity is to walk the Seawall that runs beside the bay into Stanley Park *(see p12)*, fueled with caffeine or ice cream from nearby Davie and Denman street cafés.

2 Rathtrevor Beach Provincial Park

MAP C4

Parksville's beautiful Rathtrevor Beach is easily accessible and great for watersports. Swim in the warmest saltwater north of California, build sandcastles, dig clams, canoe, or camp along the 4 miles (7 km) of sand.

3 Jericho Beach

MAP A1 ■ **Windsure Adventure Watersports: 604 224 0615**

This family-friendly beach has an outdoor shower and changing rooms for freshening up after a leisurely day of splashing around in the water. Picnics on the beach are a favorite pastime. For the more adventurous, windsurfing lessons are available at Windsure Adventure Watersports.

4 Long Beach

On the west coast of Vancouver Island, between Tofino and Ucluelet, Long Beach *(see pp32–3)* is beautiful even on a cloudy day – there are some visitors that come during the winter months specifically to watch the powerful Pacific surf pound the headland. On bright summer days, the serenity of the vast empty beach is perfect for a long stroll at low tide.

Sunset Beach in Vancouver

seaside town that shares its name. It is a great place to watch sunsets.

8 Lighthouse Park

Park in the convenient lot or hop off the bus and enjoy a short walk though West Vancouver's 500-year-old forest (see p104) to the shore. There are some breathtaking coastal views to be seen from the 1912 Point Atkinson Lighthouse. Eagle Point, on the east side of the bluff, also has stunning vistas across Burrard Inlet to Vancouver.

5 Sunset Beach

This designated quiet beach (see p83) is along the Seawall, at the mouth of False Creek. It is not far from downtown and, as the name suggests, it is a gorgeous place to watch the sun set. Vancouverites come here to watch the world go by from cafés along the waterfront, or to catch the sun on the small but lovely stretch of sand.

6 Spanish Banks Beach
MAP A2

This is the longest expanse of sandy beach in Vancouver, and is split into three sections: Spanish Bank East, Spanish Bank West, and Spanish Bank Extension. At low tide, the water can be up to 0.5 miles (1 km) off-shore. The beaches are popular with walkers, cyclists, picnickers, and families splashing in the tidal waters.

7 Qualicum Beach
MAP C4

Beachcombers and kayakers love this curved sandy beach and the

The sandy shore of Long Beach

Point Atkinson Lighthouse

9 Kitsilano Beach and Park
MAP B2 ■ Kitsilano Pool: 2305 Cornwall Ave; 604 731 0011

"Kits" Park, linked by a tree-lined walk to the beach, is favored by swimsuit-clad volleyball players and sunbathers. The busy Olympic-size Kitsilano Pool overlooks the beach.

10 Wreck Beach
MAP A4

Getting to this clothing-optional beach (see p55) is easy via a steep trail leading down from SW Marine Drive on the UBC campus. The hard part is the climb back uphill. Beware: oglers on the beach are conspicuous. There are spectacular views to be had across the Strait of Georgia towards the picturesque Vancouver Island.

Parks and Gardens

① Pacific Spirit Regional Park

This huge park on Vancouver's west side (see p104), supports pine forests as well as birch, alder, and cottonwood trees. Extensive trails cross the peninsula from Point Grey to the University of British Columbia (UBC). The park features beaches, bluffs overlooking the expansive Spanish Banks, and the Camosun Bog, an ecological treasure.

② Bloedel Conservatory

MAP B2 ▪ **Queen Elizabeth Park, W 33rd Ave & Cambie St** ▪ **604 257 8584**

Visitors to Canada's first geodesic conservatory are enveloped by steamy air as they step into this dome filled with more than 500 species of desert, tropical, and sub-tropical plants. The calls of free-flying birds complement the exotic ambience beautifully.

③ Butchart Gardens

Starting in 1904, Jenny Butchart created five spectacular gardens (see p94) to beautify her husband's excavated limestone quarry on the outskirts of Victoria. Her first creation was the elegantly manicured Japanese Garden, followed by the lush Sunken Garden. Approximately one million bedding plants blossom yearly.

Spring flowers in Beacon Hill Park

④ Beacon Hill Park

Since 1858, Beacon Hill (see p29) has been the queen of Victoria's parks. Wooden bridges built over a stream and an English-style rose garden add to the charm. Visitors can walk around, ride horses, and picnic on the beach here.

⑤ Dr. Sun Yat-Sen Classical Chinese Garden

This gem of a park (see p70) located in Chinatown reflects the serenity of a Ming Dynasty garden.

Brightly colored plants and trees in the Butchart Gardens

6 David Lam Park

MAP J5

With a large expanse of green space, this Yaletown park has lots of private corners for sitting and relaxing, as well as playgrounds and sports courts.

7 Queen Elizabeth Park

This pretty park (see p104) in central Vancouver was once a stone quarry. The Quarry Garden is now its centerpiece. A small rose garden is planted with hardy varieties that blossom year-round.

8 Stanley Park

Cedar, hemlock, and fir trees are all dotted throughout this park (see pp12–13). Old-fashioned roses and lush hybrid rhododendrons share the space with cherry, magnolia, and dog-wood trees, among others. The park staff plant 350,000 annual flowers for year-round beauty.

Geese in a pond in Vanier Park

9 Vanier Park

The English Bay serves as the backdrop for this expansive park (see p85) close to Granville Island. Largely treeless, this area was named after Georges P. Vanier, governor general of Canada from 1959 to 1967.

10 VanDusen Botanical Garden

The array of flowers, shrubs, and trees here (see p104) are unrivaled in Vancouver. Over 7,500 varieties from six continents enjoy the city's four distinct seasons. There are rolling lawns and peaceful lakes.

TOP 10 BC TREE VARIETIES

Moss-covered Douglas Fir trees

1 Douglas Fir
The province's economy was built on the lumber from this imposing tree that grows to a height of 300 ft (90 m).

2 Yellow Cedar
Growing in colder elevations, the soft wood from this tree is the ideal choice for First Nations carvings.

3 Western Red Cedar
Dark, scale-like needles mark the down-swept branches of this sometimes huge evergreen tree.

4 Hemlock
The most common tree on the West Coast, hemlock is easily recognizable by its droopy top branches.

5 Sitka Spruce
The Carmanah Giant, a Sitka spruce on Vancouver Island is, at 314 ft (95 m), the tallest recorded tree in Canada.

6 Arbutus
Peeling red-brown bark identifies the arbutus, also known as the madrona, the only broad-leafed evergreen tree native to Canada.

7 Pine
Straight lodgepole and Ponderosa pines grow at higher elevations.

8 Dogwood
The white or pink flowers of this tree bloom in spring, and famously appear on BC's official coat of arms.

9 Japanese Flowering Cherry
More than 40,000 of these blossoming trees line Vancouver's streets; many were given as a gift from Japan.

10 Maple
Canada's national tree grows in bigleaf, Douglas, and vine varieties. Bigleaf wood is often used for First Nations canoe paddles.

🔟 Children's Attractions

Visitors enjoying the fascinating exhibits at Vancouver Aquarium

1 Vancouver Aquarium
Canada's largest aquarium (see p13) introduces kids to everything from otters and penguins to tropical fish in re-created natural habitats. The on-site naturalists provide great insight into animal behavior. Special events for kids include sleepovers with sea lions.

2 H. R. MacMillan Space Centre
Children here (see p84) can touch a moon rock, watch star shows, morph into aliens, or climb aboard a spacecraft and let the motion simulator replicate the feeling of space travel.

H. R. MacMillan Space Centre

3 OMNIMAX® Theatre
Watching films on the massive five-story screen situated inside the Science World building (see pp26–7) will make children feel like they are right in the middle of the action.

4 Science World
Children can learn science in a fun way through the interactive displays at this hands-on discovery center (see pp26–7). Science World also offers healthy fast-food dining, with a special children's menu.

5 Stanley Park
The miniature railway at Stanley Park (see pp12–13) makes a fun 15-minute excursion. At Easter, Halloween, and Christmas, trains are decorated to reflect the season and themed activities are offered at the station. Kids can also play a round of golf at the pitch-and-putt course. Second Beach has a play area, a swimming pool and a beach.

6 Grouse Mountain
There's more than skiing and snowboarding at Grouse (see p101). In summer, try hiking, zip-lining, para-gliding, guided eco-walks, or riding the Skyride to the top. At the Refuge for Endangered Wildlife, visitors can see peregrine falcons, owls, and grizzlies. Loggers throw axes and roll logs at the famous lumberjack shows.

7 Granville Island Water Park

MAP H5/6 ▪ 1318 Cartwright St ▪ 604 257 8195 ▪ Open summer only (check website) ▪ www.falsecreekcc.ca

Kids will love splashing in the cool spray, shooting water cannons, and zooming down water slides at this large water park. There are changing rooms and bathrooms in the False Creek Community Centre next door.

8 Capilano Suspension Bridge Park

Walk the swaying bridge, then climb Treetops Adventure's boardwalks and platforms perched high in the forest at this park (see pp16–17).

9 Playland and the Pacific National Exhibition

MAP B2 ▪ 2901 E Hastings St ▪ Playland: open summer (hours vary, check website); adm ▪ Pacific National Exhibition: 604 253 2311; open mid-Aug–early Sep; www.pne.ca

With rides for all ages, Playland is always a hit with children. Highlights include its famed wooden roller coaster and climbing wall. During the Pacific National Exhibition, held on the same site as Playland, many additional rides are available. The fun continues year-round with a 10-day winter fair in December.

Milking activity at Maplewood Farm

10 Maplewood Farm

MAP C1 ▪ 405 Seymour River Pl ▪ 604 929 5610 ▪ Adm (free for under 18 months) ▪ www.maplewoodfarm.bc.ca

Kids can feed rabbits, learn about cow and goat-milking, and see sheep shearing demos here. There is a picnic area, a greenhouse, and an aviary, too.

TOP 10 PLACES TO EAT WITH KIDS

The Old Spaghetti Factory exterior

1 The Old Spaghetti Factory
MAP L3 ▪ 53 Water St ▪ 604 684 1288
Italian dishes are served in an old 19th century-themed warehouse.

2 Pizzeria Ludica
MAP L4 ▪ 189 Keefer Pl ▪ 604 669 5552
Diners can play one of over 700 board games at this fun-filled Italian joint.

3 Sophie's Cosmic Café
MAP G5 ▪ 2095 W 4th Ave ▪ 604 732 6810
This place has 1950s decor with booths and big portions of comfort food.

4 Rocky Mountain Flatbread Co.
MAP B2 ▪ 4186 Main St ▪ 604 566 9779
Organic pizzas and a play area for kids; parents can relax with good wine.

5 Circus Play Café
MAP B2 ▪ 1502 E Hastings St ▪ 604 558 2545
A specially designed café for families and their toddlers (admission required).

6 Go Fish
MAP H5 ▪ 1505 W 1st Ave ▪ 604 730 5040
This tiny seafood shack offers some of the best fish and chips in the city.

7 Aphrodite's
MAP A2 ▪ 3605 W 4th Ave ▪ 604 733 8308
This spot offers organic brunch and has high chairs for kids.

8 Burgoo
MAP A2 ▪ 4434 W 10th Ave ▪ 604 221 7839
This comfort food bistro, with a sunny little patio, offers a special kids' menu.

9 Sal y Limón
MAP B2 ▪ 701 Kingsway ▪ 604 677 4247
A lively café with a small play area.

10 White Spot
MAP K3 ▪ 405 Dunsmuir St ▪ 604 899 4581
Classic burgers and fries are available here, as well as healthier choices.

Entertainment Venues

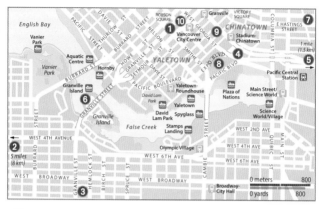

1 The Orpheum
MAP K4 ■ 601 Smithe St
■ 604 665 3035 ■ www.vancouver
civictheatres.com

Restored to Baroque grandeur, the Orpheum is a lush, former Vaudeville palace built in 1927. Musical events, including the Vancouver Symphony Orchestra, choral concerts and rock shows are performed in the acoustically upgraded space here.

Seating in Chan Shun Concert Hall

2 Chan Centre for the Performing Arts
MAP A2 ■ 6265 Crescent Rd,
University of British Columbia ■ 604
822 9197 ■ www.chancentre.com

This striking, three-venue, cylindrical center serves as a venue for music performances held in the glorious 1,200-seat Chan Shun Concert Hall,

whose adjustable acoustic canopy allows all types of music to sound their very best. A small experimental theater and a cinema round out the entertainment venues.

3 Stanley Theatre
MAP B2 ■ 2750 Granville St
■ 604 687 1644 ■ www.artsclub.com

This 1930s movie house was restored to its former elegance in the 1990s. It is now home to the Arts Club Theatre Company, who perform dramas, comedies, and musicals here.

4 Rogers Arena
MAP L4 ■ 800 Griffiths Way
Pacific Blvd N at Abbott St ■ 604 899
7400 ■ www.rogersarena.com

Home to the Vancouver Canucks National Hockey League team, this huge arena is one of the busiest entertainment venues in North America. Various concerts and events are held here regularly.

5 The Cultch
MAP B2 ■ 1895 Venables St ■
604 251 1363 ■ www.thecultch.com

Canadian and international theater and dance, as well as local and international music, are all presented in this renovated 1909 Methodist church, which now has a studio stage. The Cultch is one of the first LEED (Leadership in Energy and Environmental Design) certified arts centers in Canada.

6 Granville Island Stage/ Revue Stage

MAP H5 ■ Revue Stage: 1601 Johnston St, 604 687 1644 ■ www.artsclub.com

The Arts Club Theatre Company's 440-seat Granville Island Stage and its more intimate 198-seat Revue Stage, prove theatre doesn't have to be formal. New and classic comedies, dramas, and musicals are featured at both venues.

7 Firehall Arts Centre

MAP M3 ■ 280 E Cordova St ■ 604 689 0926 ■ www.firehallarts centre.ca

Built around 1906, this heritage fire station is now an innovative Gastown theater that features modern, and often culturally diverse plays, many by home-grown talents. The 175-seat studio theater includes an outdoor stage and a cozy, licensed lounge bar.

8 BC Place Stadium

MAP L4–L5 ■ 777 Pacific Blvd ■ 604 669 2300 ■ www.bcplace.com

This stadium features the world's largest cable-supported retractable roof. Football is the main attraction, with BC Lions games held here, as well as big concerts and trade shows.

Lights at BC Place Stadium

Concert at Queen Elizabeth Theatre

9 Queen Elizabeth Theatre and Vancouver Playhouse

MAP L4 ■ 630 Hamilton St ■ 604 665 3050 ■ www.vancouvercivic theatres.com

Home to the Vancouver Opera and Ballet BC, the Queen Elizabeth Theatre is located in a 1960s-built, Modernist venue. Adjacent to it, the Vancouver Playhouse hosts dance and music shows and events.

10 Commodore Ballroom

Since 1929, eclectic national and international acts have performed here (see p79), from Sammy Davis Jr. to The Police, U2, and Katy Perry, as well as Canadian and world music performers.

🔟 LGBTQ+ Vancouver

Patio for alfresco drinking and dining at Score on Davie

① Fountainhead Pub
MAP J4 ■ 1025 Davie St
■ 604 687 2222

With its excellent selection of lagers on tap and appetizing menu, the Fountainhead Pub is a good first stop when hitting Davie Village. It's a great place to watch sports play-offs on TV.

② Celebrities
MAP H4 ■ 1022 Davie St
■ 604 681 6180

Brilliant lighting, effects and visuals, state-of-the-art sound, and the city's hottest DJs and performers get the LGBTQ+ friendly crowd moving *(see p79)*. Apply to the online guest list and you can skip the line.

③ Score on Davie
MAP H3 ■ 1262 Davie St
■ 604 632 1646

This sports bar and grill is known for its friendly welcome, casual vibe and great patio space. It's perfect for all-day fare from tasty brunch to late-night drinks: try a Caesar (similar to a Bloody Mary cocktail) and tuck into an enormous portion of fried delights. There is also a fantastic selection of craft ales and bottled lager on offer here. Popular sports events and themed parties are hosted here regularly.

④ Pumpjack Pub
MAP H3 ■ 1167 Davie St
■ 604 685 3417

The Village's most popular LGBTQ+ pub features nightly entertainment, especially for those who are fans of the leather subculture. Drinks here are cheap, and friendly fun is guaranteed.

⑤ Delany's Coffee House
MAP H2 ■ 1105 Denman St
■ 604 662 3344

Perhaps the city's most popular see-and-be-seen coffee house, this place has a relaxed ambience and a good-sized patio.

Dancers at Celebrities nightclub

6 Little Sister's Book & Art Emporium

MAP H3 ▪ 1238 Davie St
▪ 604 669 1753

If there is an anchor to Vancouver's LGBTQ+ community, Little Sister's is it. More than a bookstore, this is an institution that has taken Canada Customs to the Supreme Court of Canada in its fight for freedom from censorship. There is a good selection of literature, event tickets, gift items, clothing, DVDs, and various adult toys.

Sunbathers on Wreck Beach

7 Sunset Beach and Wreck Beach

These two beaches are favorites of the LGBTQ+ community in Vancouver. Sunset Beach (see p83), situated a few blocks southwest of Davie Village, is popular with runners and cyclists, or those strolling with a coffee in hand. In summer, volleyball players fill up the beach. Located at the bottom of UBC cliffs, the secluded Wreck Beach (see p47) is thronged with people who enjoy sunbathing au naturel. There are several steep but maintained trails, and during the warmer months many vendors sell refreshments and beach fare.

8 Davie Village

MAP H3

With its fuchsia bus shelters and trash bins, Davie Village is the city's LGBTQ+ 'hood. Located in the West End between Burrard Street and Jervis Street, it's a lively 24-hour strip with cafés, an excellent selection of interesting shops (including sex shops), LGBTQ+ clubs, and restaurants for all budgets and tastes, not to mention its plethora of trendy bars.

9 1181

MAP J3 ▪ 1181 Davie St
▪ 236 513 1181

This sleek and modern lounge is lined with comfortable couches and illuminated with many little lights. Enjoy the extensive cocktail list served by friendly bartenders.

10 Numbers Cabaret

MAP J4 ▪ 1042 Davie St
▪ 604 685 4077

This fun, friendly, and unpretentious LGTBQ+ club is usually packed with people from all walks of life. There's something for everyone, including pool tables, darts, DJs pumping out club classics and the latest tunes across five dance floors, and also a Karaoke Funbox in the loft every night. Ongoing events at the club include cabaret nights and drag shows. Daily drinks specials feature extravagant cocktails and jugs of delicious beer.

🔟 Bars and Clubs

The award-winning patio in Lift Bar & Grill

① The Alibi Room
The go-to spot for beer aficionados, this lively tavern *(see p72)* offers an array of local craft brews. For a real west coast experience, sample an ale high in hops. Delicious pub food is also on the menu.

② The Irish Heather
This gastropub serves up good food, including many pub favorites, in a casual and friendly setting *(see p64)*. Shebeen – a whiskey house offering a great selection of more than 300 single

Exterior of Irish Heather Shebeen

malts, bourbon, rye, scotch, and whiskey – is located in this building.

③ Lift Bar & Grill
Vancouver's after-work crowd heads to this waterfront bar *(see p79)* to sip cocktails and whiskeys. Take advantage of the gorgeous views of the water, Stanley Park, and the North Shore from several levels of patios, all comfortably heated when the temperatures drop. Happy hour is from 3pm to 6pm every day.

④ Botanist
A chic, modern bar and restaurant *(see p79)* situated in the Fairmont Pacific Rim hotel, the Botanist serves innovative brunch cocktails such as the Pacific Mist, made with gin, Earl Grey tea, honey, and egg white. Be sure to try the food too, which is crafted with fresh Pacific Northwest ingredients.

⑤ The Bimini
2010 W 4th Ave ▪ 604 564 7114
Enjoy modern pub food and local craft beers at this well-established pub in the Kitsilano neighborhood. The dance floor gets lively with locals

in the evening. You can also watch live sports on big-screen TVs and play arcade games and pool.

6 The Keefer Bar
With a patio and a funky decor, this swanky and sleek cocktail bar (see p72) in Chinatown is the perfect place to unwind. It offers medicinal-sounding drinks and Asian inspired cocktails alongside late-night dim sum snacks and fusion small plates. The music is a mix of soul, hip-hop, and funk, and it also features live music.

7 Commodore Ballroom
Established back in 1926, the Commodore Ballroom (see p79) has seen many musical eras. Catch one of the many great acts and test out the ballroom's bouncy sprung floor. Updated, and always on the cutting edge of music, this venue lives on as the city's great-grandfather of clubs.

8 Guilt & Co.
This cool little place (see p72) hosts nightly live performances in an easily missed basement venue beneath the Local in Gastown. Make sure you get there early as they operate a one-in-one-out policy to avoid over-crowding. Indulge in some great cocktails and choose from their extensive whiskey menu.

Legendary club The Roxy

9 The Roxy
A Vancouver institution, The Roxy (see p79) hosts top Canadian and local bands, and is a favorite nightspot of some local sports teams. Line-ups at this popular club are common after 9pm, so be warned and get in line early.

10 Granville Island Brewing
The taproom at the center of the brewery (see pp24–5) that started Vancouver's love of small-batch handcrafted beer is on bustling Granville Island. Since 1984 the brewery has consistently promoted the use of natural ingredients and West Coast inspiration – they'll even advise you on the best beers to drink along with the delicious food offered at the venue, which is made exclusively using local produce.

Beer from Granville Island Brewing

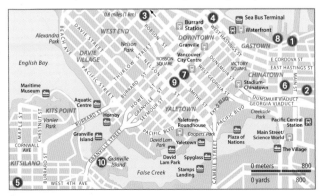

🔟 Restaurants

Interior at Blue Water Café

1 Blue Water Café

The freshest and finest wild seafood is served in a 100-year-old brick-and-beam warehouse *(see p89)*. The decor is contemporary, the atmosphere friendly, and the kitchen serves mouthwatering delicacies such as sablefish in soy and ginger broth. The Raw Bar at this café is the domain of a master sushi chef.

2 Miku

This Japanese restaurant *(see p73)* is known for its gourmet *Aburi* (flame-seared sushi), complemented by an elegant setting.

Beautifully presented food at Chambar

Traditional Japanese flavors and techniques combined with West Coast elements create an innovative menu, with sustainable seafood recognized by the Ocean Wise conservation program. It has a bar, lounge area and full-service sushi bar.

3 Tacofino

With humble beginnings as a food truck in Tofino on the west coast of Vancouver Island, this taco hotspot *(see p73)* has several outlets, including one in Gastown's Blood Alley. You can tuck into delicious and filling burritos, or sip margaritas and craft beers on the sunny patio. The menu also offers a range of tacos, nachos, and churros. They also feature daily happy hour specials from 3pm to 6pm.

4 Chambar

Success hasn't spoiled this Belgian restaurant in the Crosstown neighborhood *(see p73)*. It is one of the hottest eateries in town and perennially packed to the rafters. Traditional dishes such as *moules frites* excel, but for a real treat try the *Congolaise* version, where mussels are cooked in a tomato and coconut cream sauce with smoked chili and lime.

Softly lit dining area at CinCin Ristorante & Bar

5 CinCin Ristorante & Bar

The Italian-inspired menu of this inviting space *(see p81)* includes dishes from the wood-fired oven. If you're not in a rush, order the melt-in-your-mouth free-range chicken cooked under a brick in the wood-fired oven for 25 minutes. The drinks menu lists more than 1,000 wines.

6 Bao Bei

Locals rave about the lamb sirloin sliders, heavenly dumplings, and innovative small plates at this Chinese brasserie *(see p73)*. Bao Bei does not take reservations, so arrive early. With advance notice, groups of eight to ten can enjoy a tasting menu at the large family table.

7 Diva at the Met

A modern and spacious restaurant *(see p81)* with fine Pacific Northwest-influenced dishes, such as wild caught halibut with risotto, as well as vegan dishes. The brunch here is great too.

8 Forage

If you're seeking a healthy and hearty meal, then Forage *(see p81)* is the place to go. With an emphasis on local, organic and sustainably-sourced ingredients, this casual restaurant offers a range of creative dishes. Book a family table menu, or try out their brunches, which feature exceptional fare such as corned bison hash.

9 Hawksworth

Situated in an elegant room at the Rosewood Hotel Georgia, this gem *(see p81)* has garnered multiple awards for its dazzling food and star chef David Hawksworth. The *foie gras*, roasted lamb, and rib-eye steak dishes are all outstanding in terms of presentation and flavor.

Plush dining tables at the Hawksworth

10 Cioppino's Mediterranean Grill

Inventive *cucina*-style dishes *(see p89)* are made with fresh vegetables and low-fat sauces for a healthy meal. The succulent natural beef short ribs braised in red wine is excellent too. A great wine list and leafy patio rounds out the experience.

🔟 Shopping Destinations

Interior of the huge Metropolis at Metrotown

1 Metropolis at Metrotown

MAP C2 ■ 4700 Kingsway, Burnaby ■ 604 438 4715

This is BC's largest mall. The atmosphere is lively with many shoppers visiting daily. The Hudson's Bay department store and the grocery giant Superstore anchor the mall, with chains and independents represented by more than 400 stores. There are movie screens and arcade games for non-shoppers.

2 Robson Street

The trendy Robson Street's shopping epicenter (see p76) is situated at the corner of Burrard and Robson, where the stylish brands Lululemon and Roots Canada make their homes. Shop for clothing at another Canadian store, Aritzia, pick up indulgent bath products in Lush, or browse the several internationally known shoe, clothing, accessory, and home furnishing stores. You can catch a breather at any of the numerous restaurants en route.

3 South Granville

MAP H6

In South Granville, shopping extends along Granville Street from 2nd to 16th avenues. Nearly a dozen art galleries can be found here. The elegant strip is home to brand-name and high-end European clothing purveyors such as Bacci's, Boboli (see p87), and also Max Mara. Excellent tea and coffee shops, home decor showrooms, and some toy stores are peppered along this strip as well.

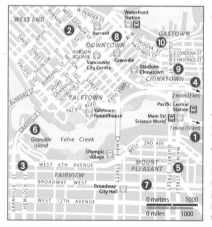

4 Commercial Drive

MAP B2

The Drive, as it's known locally, is the epitome of a hip area. Vancouver's Little Italy, it is a multicultural fusion of clothing shops, book and magazine stores, vintage boutiques, and second-hand outlets. To make the most of your visit here, start off at East Broadway and Commercial Drive and walk northward to Venables Street, admiring the magnificent Coast Mountains that appear in the distance along the way.

5 **Mount Pleasant**
MAP M6

From 2nd Avenue to 22nd Avenue, along Main Street, a wonderful assortment of independent boutiques line this Mount Pleasant neighborhood. After filling your shopping bags full of vintage treasures, books, and hand-crafted stationery, stop by one of the many breweries and coffee shops for refreshments.

6 **Granville Island**
There's more to shopping on the Island than just fresh foods at the Public Market: look for silver jewelry and hats among the stalls *(see p86)*. The Net Loft – once used for fishing net repairs – sells crafts and handmade paper. The Kids Market offers a host of mini-shops and activities for the little ones.

Stall at Granville Island Public Market

7 **Broadway**
MAP A1–B1

Shopping hotspots on Broadway are located between Main and Alma streets. Scattered along the street are various clothing stores such as Plenty, a local favorite selling stylish clothing and accessories. Health food stores are also dotted along the street, particularly at Granville, Arbutus, and Macdonald streets (the latter is home to the city's Greektown).

8 **Pacific Centre**
MAP K3 ▪ 701 W Georgia St
▪ 604 688 7235

More than 100 stores stretch beneath Granville Street in the heart of downtown Vancouver, including department stores, boutiques, and specialty stores selling clothing, jewelry, sportswear, gadgets, and more.

Shopping street in Chinatown

9 **Chinatown**
One of Vancouver's oldest and largest shopping areas *(see p70)* has struggled at times to survive with competition from Richmond's Asian supermalls. Yet Chinatown hangs on, its crowded streets filled with bargain hunters. Shops selling herbs and potions, fresh seafood and vegetables, leather goods, and Asian souvenirs fill the streets.

10 **Gastown**
The century-old buildings of Gastown *(see p69)* have morphed into unique boutiques, First Nations art galleries, and specialty shops selling everything from buttons to cowboy boots. Gastown has long been known for its souvenirs, and many retailers line Water Street, selling classic as well as kitsch Canadiana.

Cowboy boots in a shop in Gastown

🔟 Vancouver and Vancouver Island for Free

Art Deco detail in the Marine Building

1 Marine Building
MAP K3 ■ 355 Burrard St
Close to Canada Place (which can of course also be explored for free), this 1930s building is adored by those in the know. It was once the tallest building across the British Empire, with mesmerizing Art Deco details in the grand entrance, lobby, and elevators. Entrance to the lobby is free on weekdays between 8:30am and 5pm.

2 The Seawall
The city's famed greenway (see p12) offers epic views, great picnic spots, and beaches along its 17.5-mile (28-km) route. The stretch around Stanley Park is one-way only.

3 The Grouse Grind
A challenging hike with rewarding views, the Grouse Grind in North Vancouver is free to get to by shuttle from Canada Place to Grouse Mountain.

British Columbia Parliament Buildings

4 Christ Church Cathedral
With the motto "Open Doors, Open Hearts, Open Minds" Christ Church Cathedral (see p75) can be visited for free all week, but Choral Eucharist (at 10:30am on Sundays) is when the custom-built Kenneth Jones organ and the award-winning choir can be heard.

5 Free Walking Tours
City of Vancouver: www.vancouver.ca ■ Vancouver DeTours: www.vancouverdetours.ca
There are several downloadable brochures for fascinating self-guided public art walking tours available on the City of Vancouver website. You can also book free city walking tours on the Vancouver DeTours website (although the guides do appreciate a tip at the end of the tour).

6 British Columbia Parliament Buildings
Victoria's imposing Neo-Classical 19th-century Parliament building (see p28) is home to the Legislative Assembly of British Columbia. Free public tours run on weekdays when Parliament isn't sitting (check the website for times) and you don't need to book beforehand. However, for speciality tours that focus on the architecture or formal gardens, you will have to reserve a place in advance.

7 Lynn Canyon Park

This expansive park (see p102) is a lush green space with walking trails and swimming holes, plus a 50-m (165-ft) suspension bridge. The entire site, including the ecology center, can be visited free of charge.

8 International Buddhist Temple

MAP B3 ■ 9160 Steveston Hwy, Richmond (25 mins from downtown) ■ www.buddhisttemple.ca

Chinese culture and heritage, and Buddhist philosophy, is celebrated at Richmond's International Buddhist Temple (see p103), which is open to all. Don't miss the formal gardens, which can also be explored for free.

International Buddhist Temple

9 Free Admission

Some of the finest museums and galleries throw open their doors for free on certain days (a donation of whatever you can afford is appreciated). Head to the Bill Reid Gallery (see p77) from 2pm to 5pm then Vancouver Art Gallery (see p20–21) from 4pm to 8pm on the first Friday of the month.

10 Free Festivals and Events

Vancouver and the surrounding area host free festivals and events in every season, such as the world's largest fireworks festival, an open-air concert at the end of the jazz festival, and Pride (see pp64–5). Summer street parties, hosted by the Mural Festival and Public Disco are also popular. On December evenings, watch for the Carol Ships Parade of Lights in Coal Harbour, when dozens of boats are decorated in festive lights.

TOP 10 BUDGET TIPS

Beacon Hill Park in Victoria

1 Spend time taking it easy for free in the excellent parks and gardens (see pp48–9) in Vancouver and Victoria.

2 Some of the best afternoon and early evening happy hours are at The Keefer Bar (see p78), The Flying Pig (see p89), and L'Abattoir (see p73).

3 Save money on public transit costs in the city by buying all-zone day passes, or by getting a reloadable Compass Card.

4 Take the Canada Line from the airport to downtown for less than $10.

5 Visit and explore year-round farmers' markets (www.eatlocal.org) that are free and offer inexpensive food options.

6 T&T supermarket is the place to stock up on inexpensive Asian staples and they often have free samples (www.tntsupermarket.com).

7 For cheap dining, find out where the city's best food trucks are (www.streetfoodapp.com/vancouver).

8 A Vancouver City Passport ($29.95) offers money-off coupons for major tourist attractions (www.citypassports.com).

9 Travel the city using the Mobi bike share scheme. Riders can pick up a bicycle at many convenient locations across the city (www.mobibikes.ca).

10 Sign up with Hostelling International before you travel to get access to all the best value hostels (www.hihostels.com). Unaffiliated hotels do sometimes offer discounts for members, too.

Festivals and Events

1 Lunar New Year
Jan–Feb ■ www.lunarfest
vancouver.ca
Vancouver is filled with celebrations
each Lunar New Year, with a massive
parade moving through Chinatown.

2 Vancouver International Wine Festival
604 872 6623 ■ Late Feb–early Mar
■ www.vanwinefest.ca
From humble beginnings in 1979,
the VanWineFest now hosts premier
industry names and is considered
to be one of the biggest, oldest, and
the best wine events in the world.
It features tastings, gourmet dinners,
seminars, and culinary competitions.

3 Bard on the Beach Shakespeare Festival
MAP G4 ■ Vanier Park ■ 604 739 0559
■ Jun–late Sep ■ www.bardonthe
beach.org
Western Canada's largest professional
Shakespeare festival, Bard on the
Beach presents plays by the Bard
and other events such as operas,
firework displays, and even seminars
and talks.

4 Concord Pacific Dragon Boat Festival
False Creek ■ 604 688 2382 ■ Mid-Jun
■ www.concorddragonboatfestival.ca
Over 5,500 paddlers from around the
world gather for a weekend of fun.

There's more to do than just watch
the races. Food stalls, interactive
exhibits, entertaining music shows,
and cultural installations abound.

The Jazz Festival in full swing

5 Vancouver International Jazz Festival
604 872 5200 ■ Late Jun–early Jul
■ www.coastaljazz.ca
One of the largest music festivals in
all of Canada, the International Jazz
Festival features some 400 concerts
around town wherein jazz in every
imaginable style is presented. Per-
formance venues include galleries,
bars, restaurants, and nightclubs.
Many parks and open spaces across
the city also serve as venues for free
concerts. The event wraps up with
an outdoor multistage free weekend.

6 Vancouver Folk Music Festival
MAP A1 ■ Jericho
Beach Park ■ 604
602 9798 ■ Mid-Jul
■ www.thefestival.
bc.ca
International and
Canadian acts play on
open-air stages. The
waterside park hosts
nearly 30,000 folk music
fanatics for three eve-
nings and two full days
of non-stop music.

Concord Pacific Dragon Boat Festival

⑦ Honda Celebration of Light

Late Jul ▪ www.hondacelebration
oflight.com

Night skies fill with fireworks, accompanied by music, as three countries compete to win top bragging rights. Crowds flock to English Bay, Vanier Park, Jericho, Kitsilano, and West Vancouver beaches, so go early in order to snag a good spot.

⑧ Vancouver Pride Festival

604 687 0955 ▪ Late Jul–early
Aug ▪ www.vancouverpride.ca

For two weeks, the LGBTQ+ community gathers in the city's West End to celebrate. The festival is a bevy of picnics, dances, cruises, breakfasts, and a grand finale parade and beach party.

⑨ Vancouver International Film Festival

604 683 3456 ▪ Early Oct
▪ www.viff.org

More than 150,000 people attend this annual festival. Films from Canada and the Pacific Rim are screened.

A screening at the Film Festival

⑩ Vancouver Writers Fest

MAP H5 ▪ Granville Island
▪ 604 681 6330 ▪ Mid-Oct ▪ www.
writersfest.bc.ca

International and Canadian writers attract throngs of readers to forums, readings, and literary cabarets in English and French. Writers stay on the festival site, so there's a decent chance you'll get to meet and chat with a celebrity author.

TOP 10 PERFORMING GROUPS

1 Firehall Arts Centre
This theater group (see p53) puts on entertaining shows, often with a multicultural twist.

2 Ballet BC
Ticketmaster: 1-855-985-2787
World-class ballet shows are performed under bold leadership.

3 Vancouver Recital Society
604 602 0363
The Vancouver Recital Society has a reputation for innovation and excellence in its programming.

4 Vancouver Opera
604 683 0222
This famous company puts on grand-scale productions of traditional and contemporary pieces.

5 The Dance Centre
604 606 6400
Traditional and contemporary dance performances from around the globe.

6 Early Music Vancouver
604 732 1610
The group plays concerts of works by medieval to late-Romantic composers.

7 Arts Club Theatre Company
Contemporary drama is performed by this group at Granville Island Stage and the Stanley Theatre (see pp52–3).

8 Vancouver Theatresports League
604 738 7013
A great improv-based comedy group at Granville Island's Improv Centre.

9 Kokoro Dance
604 662 7441
Distorted movement and great intensity characterize Kokoro's butoh, a postwar Japanese dance form.

10 Vancouver Symphony Orchestra
604 876 3434
This wonderful orchestra performs world-class orchestral music.

Vancouver Symphony Orchestra

Vancouver and Vancouver Island Area by Area

The Lost Lagoon at Stanley Park and Vancouver Skyline

🔟 Waterfront, Gastown, and Chinatown

The Waterfront is Vancouver's heart, and is one of the largest and busiest ports on the continent. With the opening of the cruise-ship terminal at Canada Place in the mid-1980s, it also became one of the world's major cruise-ship ports. A block away is Gastown, its origin as a mill town masked by graceful heritage buildings constructed in the boom years of the early 1900s. From here it is just a short walk to Chinatown, now home to some of Vancouver's best restaurants and bars. However, its prosperity did not come easily – the immigrant population was once seen as a threat by local workers, and a closed-door immigration policy was imposed in 1885. Today, Chinatown attracts many shoppers seeking Chinese food and souvenirs.

Steam Clock, Gastown

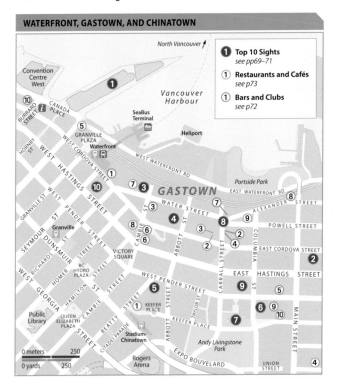

WATERFRONT, GASTOWN, AND CHINATOWN

1 **Top 10 Sights**
see pp69–71

1 **Restaurants and Cafés**
see p73

1 **Bars and Clubs**
see p72

Canada Place, with its five sails, lit up at dusk

1 Canada Place

When the now iconic Canada Place *(see pp14–15)* opened back in 1986, it was greeted with controversy. Critics said its five "sails" were a poor imitation of Australia's Sydney Opera House. Today, the landmark complex is a key player on the waterfront that has grown up around it.

2 Vancouver Police Museum

MAP M4 ■ 240 E Cordova St ■ 604 665 3346 ■ Open 11am–5pm Thu–Sat (from noon Sun) ■ Adm ■ www. vancouverpolicemuseum.ca

Housed in the former Coroner Court and built in 1932, this museum *(see p41)* traces the fascinating history and operations of the Vancouver Police Department. Real examples of criminal evidence are exhibited, including counterfeit money, antique firearms, and street weaponry. Always popular among museum visitors is the knife room. Unsolved murders are depicted in displays, complete with dummies and period costumes.

3 Steam Clock

MAP L3 ■ Water St at Cambie St

Said to be the first steam-operated clock in the world, this landmark is one of the most photographed spots in the city. However, the clock is not an antique. Local horologist Raymond Saunders built this 16-ft- (5-m-) tall clock in 1977 at the corner of Water

and Cambie streets, basing it on an 1875 model. Be patient, and wait to hear the Westminster Quarters chime melody that plays every 15 minutes, along with mighty puffs of steam that billow from its five whistles.

4 Gastown

MAP L3–M3

The cobblestone streets of Gastown have been through many reincarnations. Since the 1970s, this area has seen considerable renovation. The plethora of tawdry souvenir shops have largely been replaced with boutiques selling the work of local designers, a concentration of excellent First Nations and Inuit art galleries, and a great selection of restaurants and clubs.

Boutiques lining a street in Gastown

AN IRON ROAD, COAST TO COAST

The grand saga of Canadian railways is a tale of power and pain. In 1886, Prime Minister John A. Macdonald fulfilled his promise to build a cross-Canada railway to unite the new Dominion of Canada. The first transcontinental passenger train arrived in Vancouver on May 23, 1887, where Waterfront Station now stands. The whole city came out to celebrate the completion of the "Iron Road." Even the ships in the harbor were decked out in flags. Sadly, progress came at the loss of many lives, including more than 600 Chinese laborers.

Dr. Sun Yat-Sen Chinese Garden

⑤ Sun Tower

MAP L4 ■ 100 W Pender St

A Vancouver landmark, the 17-story Sun Tower was the tallest building in the British Commonwealth, at 270 ft (82 m), when it was built in 1911. The handsome Beaux Arts building's nine nude statues once scandalized the city, but people turned out in droves in 1918 to watch Harry Gardiner, the "Human Fly," scale its walls.

⑥ Chinatown

MAP L4–M4

Stretching from Gore Avenue west to Carrall Street between Pender and Keefer streets, Chinatown dates to the 1880s and the building of the Canadian Pacific Railway, when as many as 20,000 Chinese came to Canada. Today, this neighborhood is North America's third-largest Chinatown. The Millennium Gate straddles Pender Street and is an ideal place to start a walking tour of this lively area.

⑦ Dr. Sun Yat-Sen Classical Chinese Garden

MAP M4 ■ 578 Carrall St ■ 604 662 3207 ■ Adm ■ www.vancouver chinesegarden.com

This Ming Dynasty-style garden, the first built outside China, opened in 1986. It re-creates the private areas typically found in a Ming scholar's home. With its meandering paths, corridors and courtyards, and asymmetrically placed rocks, the garden invites contemplation on the beauty and rhythm of nature.

⑧ Maple Tree Square

MAP M3 ■ Water St at Carrall St

The city of Vancouver has its roots in this small square. The publican and Gastown's founder, John "Gassy Jack" Deighton, built the city's first saloon with the help of local sawmill workers. A maple tree here once marked a popular meeting place until it was destroyed in

Maple Tree Square, Gastown

the Great Fire of 1886. Gaoler's Mews was the site of the city's first prison, as well as the home of the city's first policeman, Constable Jonathan Miller.

9 Chinese Canadian Museum

MAP M4 ■ 51 E Pender ■ 604 262 0990 ■ Open 10am–5pm Wed–Sat ■ Adm; under-5s free

When the Chinese Exclusion Act paused immigration from China in 1923, it cut off ties between labourers and their families back home. This museum is now shedding light on this oft-overlooked part of the country's history, while celebrating Chinese Canadian art and culture.

The towering Vancouver Lookout

10 Vancouver Lookout

MAP L3 ■ 555 W Hastings St ■ 604 689 0421 ■ Open 10am–7pm daily ■ Adm; under-5s free

The highlight of the Harbour Centre complex is its 581-ft (177-m) tower, home to an observation deck. The ride up in the glass-fronted elevator takes a thrilling 40 seconds. From the enclosed observation deck, the 360-degree view is splendid. On a clear day, you can see Vancouver Island to the west and Washington State's snow-capped Mount Baker to the south.

A DAY IN WATERFRONT, GASTOWN, AND CHINATOWN

▶ MORNING

Begin your day at **Canada Place** *(see p69)* for an excellent view of the harbor. After strolling the promenade for about half an hour, walk east towards historic **Gastown**. From the junction of Cordova and Water streets, continue two blocks along Water Street to Cambie Street to admire the **Steam Clock** *(see p69)*, then stop at the hip café **Revolver** *(see p73)* for coffee. Enjoy an architectural walking tour around Gastown's heritage buildings, before heading off to **Tacofino** *(see p73)* for lunch.

AFTERNOON

Walk down to **Maple Tree Square**, at Water and Carrall streets, to see the bronze statue of "Gassy Jack," the famous proprietor of the city's first saloon. From East Cordova, head south on Carrall Street to the peaceful **Dr. Sun Yat-Sen Classical Chinese Garden**. Spend 30 minutes here, then continue to the fascinating Chinese Canadian Museum *(see p40)*. Head east on Pender Street, admiring **Millennium Gate** as you walk through it into Chinatown. Spend the rest of the afternoon exploring the shops, looking out for the wooden heritage buildings you pass. End the day feasting on delicious modern Chinese food at **Bao Bei** *(see p73)* and then sip cocktails at **The Keefer Bar** *(see p72)*, where you can listen to DJs spinning the latest tunes.

See map on p68 ←

Bars and Clubs

Homely bar and dining area at Steamworks Brewing

1 Steamworks Brewing
MAP L3 ■ 375 Water St
■ 604 689 2739

Complement your pizza, pasta, burger, or poutine with one of the several delicious beers brewed here, especially the seasonal selections.

2 The Irish Heather
MAP M4 ■ 248 E Georgia St
■ 604 688 9779

There are about 200 single malts and Irish whiskeys to pick from in this pub (see p56). Menu favorites include bangers 'n' mash.

3 The Pourhouse
MAP L3 ■ 162 Water St
■ 604 568 7022

This evocative 1910 venue is steeped in history. It has low lighting, a chilled ambience, as well as a range of clever cocktails and pub food.

4 The Blarney Stone
MAP M4 ■ 216 Carrall St
■ 604 687 4322

Friday and Saturday nights guarantee a rip-roaring, feet-stomping crowd at this legendary Irish pub and nightclub.

5 Fortune Sound Club
MAP M4 ■ 147 E Pender St
■ Open hours vary, check website
■ www.fortunesoundclub.com

This Chinatown hotspot is famous for its hip-hop weekend club nights along with indie and electronic music shows.

6 The Cambie
MAP L3 ■ 300 Cambie St
■ 604 688 9158

Pouring drinks since 1887, The Cambie is legendary and features a lively hostel upstairs. Cheap microbrews are the big draw.

7 Guilt & Co.
MAP M3 ■ 1 Alexander St
■ 604 288 1704

This dimly lit underground live music venue (see p57) features refined but unfussy food and drinks. Visit to see a daily rotation of local music bands – no tickets required.

8 Alibi Room
MAP M3 ■ 157 Alexander St
■ 604 623 3383

DJs play funk, soul, and hip-hop in this two-level space with craft beers on tap, making it a top spot to sample an array of local brews.

9 The Keefer Bar
MAP M4 ■ 135 Keefer St
■ 604 688 1961

Nestled in the heart of Chinatown, this cocktail bar (see p57) serves creative drinks and snacks.

10 Lobby Lounge
MAP L3 ■ 1038 Canada Pl
■ 604 695 5300

See and be seen at the Fairmont Pacific Rim's stylish lounge bar, which features live music by local artists.

Restaurants and Cafés

1 Chambar
MAP L4 ▪ 568 Beatty St
▪ 604 879 7119 ▪ $$$

Moules frites are the specialty at this hugely popular Belgian restaurant *(see p58)*, where the cocktail menu is a great way to start the evening.

2 Tacofino
MAP L3 ▪ 15 W Cordova St
▪ 604 899 7907 ▪ $

This Mexican-inspired restaurant *(see p58)*, which has grown up fast since its days as a food truck in Tofino, still serves the original fish taco that is considered the best in town.

3 L'Abattoir
MAP M4 ▪ 217 Carrall St
▪ 604 568 1701 ▪ Closed L ▪ $$$

L'Abattoir offers fine dining in an informal setting of refurbished brick and beam. The menu has French-influenced West Coast fare at its best. The weekend brunch is exquisite.

Chic interior of L'Abattoir

4 Harvest Community Foods
MAP M4 ▪ 243 Union St ▪ 604 682 8851 ▪ $

A Chinatown grocery store and café stocked with fresh, local farm produce. Try the ramen noodle soups, or pick up cheeses and baked goods.

PRICE CATEGORIES
For a three-course meal for one with half a bottle of wine (or equivalent meal), taxes, and extra charges.
....
$ under $35 $$ $35–85 $$$ over $85

---

5 Miku
MAP L3 ▪ Suite 70–200 Granville St ▪ 604 568 3900 ▪ $$$

With an atmospheric waterfront setting, this Japanese restaurant *(see p58)* offers fresh, sustainable fish, specializing in flame-seared *Aburi* sushi.

6 Meat & Bread
MAP L3 ▪ 370 Cambie St
▪ 604 566 9003 ▪ Closed D ▪ $

The excellent sandwiches served here draw crowds, so expect long, yet fast-moving queues during lunch.

7 Al Porto Ristorante
MAP L3 ▪ 321 Water St
▪ 604 683 8376 ▪ $$

Pastas, fish, meat, and pizza are the highlights at this lively Italian *trattoria*. More than 300 wines are on offer.

8 Revolver
MAP L3 ▪ 325 Cambie St
▪ 604 558 4444 ▪ Closed D, Sun ▪ $

Baristas who are deadly serious about the roasting and brewing process serve coffee in this trendy exposed-brick café. Try the brew flight – a selection of amazing espressos.

9 The Birds & The Beets
MAP M3 ▪ 55 Powell St
▪ 604 893 7832 ▪ Closed D ▪ $

This cozy café uses organic and local ingredients to serve simple dishes, including lovely avocado on toast.

10 Bao Bei
MAP M4 ▪ 163 Keefer St
▪ 604 688 0876 ▪ Closed L ▪ $$

In Bao Bei's sophisticated dining room *(see p59)*, a savvy take on Chinese home cooking is the order of the day. Start with one of the expertly crafted cocktails available at the bar.

See map on p68 ←

TOP 10 Downtown

Originally a logging settlement surrounded by swamps, mills, and a few taverns, Vancouver's Downtown core has transformed and emerged as a sophisticated urban landscape with gleaming office towers, luxury boutiques, bustling shopping malls, and outstanding restaurants. The wide streets are lined with grand landmark buildings, vintage theaters, and fine art galleries. Downtown is always alive with a frenetic pace of activity, while the well-dressed locals rush about to relax and finish their day with a cocktail at one of the happening neighborhood lounges. Extending from Stanley Park and the West End to the west, to the historic districts of Gastown and Chinatown to the east, this area can be easily explored on foot.

Haida artist Bill Reid's totem pole at Brockton Point, Stanley Park

DOWNTOWN

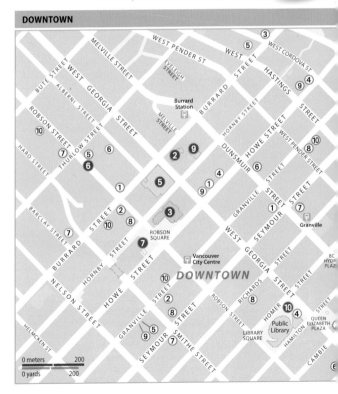

1 Stanley Park

This 1.6 sq miles (4 sq km) of tamed wilderness is the green lungs of the city. The park *(see pp12–13)* is crisscrossed with trails and cultural landmarks, including Coast Salish gateways, totems at Brockton Point, and the life-size sculpture *Girl in a Wetsuit*. The Seawall circumnavigates it all and provides a perfect space for walking and cycling with stunning ocean views.

Interior of Christ Church Cathedral

2 Christ Church Cathedral
MAP K3 ■ 690 Burrard St
■ 604 682 3848

A gem in the heart of the city and once a beacon for mariners entering

Greater Vancouver

0 km   2
0 miles   2

Stanley Park ①

Lost Lagoon

Burrard Inlet

English Bay

⑤ ④ ③

③ *Area of main map*

WEST END

③

⑥ ⑨

Vanier Park

⑧ CHINATOWN

② YALETOWN

False Creek ④

GRANVILLE

VICTORY SQUARE

STREET

BEATTY ST

CITADEL PARADE

Vancouver's harbor, Christ Church Cathedral, consecrated in 1895, was designed in the Gothic Revival style. The church interior has impressive old-growth Douglas fir ceiling beams and 32 stunning stained-glass windows; three in the office vestibule are by the British artist William Morris. Outside stands a 100-ft (30-m) tower of steel, clad with stained glass by Canadian artist Sarah Hall.

Big Raven, **Vancouver Art Gallery**

3 Vancouver Art Gallery

When the Court House was erected in 1912, designed by Francis Rattenbury, one of BC's flashiest architects, its solid form symbolized the British Empire at its very peak. Another controversial architect, Arthur Erickson, supervised the building's redesign in the mid-1980s when it became the Vancouver Art Gallery *(see pp20–21)*. Inside, the Emily Carr collection is Canada's largest, and includes the work *Big Raven*. Contemporary photoconceptual work also has a prominent place.

4 Science World

The striking geodesic dome housing Science World's interactive galleries and traveling exhibitions (see pp26–7) was built for Expo '86. Visitors can play with magnetic liquids, check out exhibits on motion and energy, and also watch superb laser shows. The OMNIMAX® Theatre's screen fits into the dome's curves.

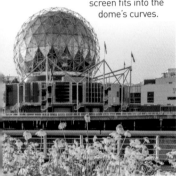

Futuristic exterior of Science World

5 Fairmont Hotel Vancouver

MAP K3 ■ 900 W Georgia St ■ 604 684 3131 ■ www.fairmont.com

Begun in 1928 by the Canadian Pacific Railway, construction on the city's most famous hotel halted with the 1929 stock market crash. Its steel skeleton sat until 1939, when it was hastily finished for the visit of King George VI. Features include a steep copper roof with impish gargoyles. Stroll through the lobby and enjoy afternoon tea or a drink in the lounge, while admiring the lavish surrounds.

6 Robson Street

MAP H2–K4

West End residents, the city's urban chic, international celebrities, and tourists alike flock to Robson Street to join the bustle of shoppers (see p60). Part of the fun is people-watching over a specialty coffee, then browsing the brand-name and independent Canadian and international shops. Slip down a side street to get a taste of the historic West End, Canada's most densely populated area.

7 Robson Square and Law Courts

MAP J4 ■ 800 block Robson St ■ 604 660 8989

Spanning several blocks and four levels, Robson Square was designed by BC architect Arthur Erickson. The surrounding pedestrian plaza features a cascading waterfall fountain and often hosts food trucks, making it popular with local office workers. In the winter, a public skating rink takes over the area.

Cascading waterfall in Robson Square

TERRY FOX'S MARATHON OF HOPE

Born in Winnipeg in 1958, Terry Fox grew up in a Vancouver suburb. When just 18 years old, he was diagnosed with bone cancer and had his leg amputated. Three years later, in 1980, Terry dipped his artificial leg into the Atlantic, starting his Marathon of Hope across Canada to raise money for cancer research. After 143 days and 3,339 miles (5,373 km) Terry stopped. The cancer had spread to his lungs and he died in 1981, just after realizing his dream of raising $1 for every Canadian – over $24 million. A memorial to Terry Fox now stands at BC Place.

BC Sports Hall of Fame and Museum

(8) BC Sports Hall of Fame and Museum

MAP L4 ▪ 777 Pacific Blvd S, Gate A ▪ Adm ▪ www.bcsportshall.com

Twenty galleries showcase BC's sports history from the 1860s onward in a 20,000-sq-ft (1,858-sq-m) space located in BC Place Stadium (see p53). Interactive displays provide fascinating details of the lives of famous athletes, such as skier Nancy Green and sprinter Harry Jerome. The Participation Gallery is especially fun for kids.

(9) Bill Reid Gallery

MAP K3 ▪ 639 Hornby St ▪ 604 682 3455 ▪ Open May–Sep: 10am–5pm daily; Oct–Apr: 11am–5pm Wed–Sun ▪ www.billreidgallery.ca

Haida artist, master carver and gold- and silversmith Bill Reid blazed a trail for First Nations artists. The public gallery (see p41) named after him is home to contemporary Indigenous Northwest Coast art, and temporary exhibits are thoughtful and far-reaching. A permanent gallery of his works, "Restoring Enchantment," exhibits a 28-ft (8.5-m) bronze frieze.

(10) Library Square

MAP K4 ▪ Corner of Robson & Homer sts

The Vancouver Central Library, partly designed by famed architect Moshe Safdie, opened in 1995. At first criticized by some for its resemblance to a Roman amphitheater, it soon became universally popular. Today, the Library Square takes up a whole city block, and includes the library, the Federal Tower housing government offices, a glass-roofed promenade, shops, restaurants, and a rooftop garden.

A DOWNTOWN WALK

Vancouver Art Gallery — Pacific Centre — Gotham Steakhouse
Robson Square
Robson Street — Library Square
Terry Fox Memorial — BC Sports Hall of Fame and Museum
BC Place Stadium

▶ MORNING

Start at BC Place Stadium (see p53), exploring the BC Sports Hall of Fame and Museum for about an hour. Exiting the museum, head west towards Robson Street, passing by the four bronze statues of the Terry Fox Memorial, each bigger than the last, a tribute to the local hero who raised millions of dollars for cancer research. Continue west three blocks along Robson towards Homer Street and Library Square. Drop in to have a look at the building's airy promenade before walking westwards to Pacific Centre (see p61). Browse the shops until lunchtime, then exit the mall and cross Howe Street to Vancouver Art Gallery (see pp20–21). Enjoy a salad and sandwich in its 1931 Gallery Bistro (604 662 4831), snagging a patio table if the weather permits.

AFTERNOON

After lunch, head to the fourth floor of the Vancouver Art Gallery and take in the wonderful Emily Carr collection. Begin by watching the 15-minute video about this remarkable painter of forests and totem poles. Exiting the gallery, cross Robson and stroll through lovely Robson Square. Afterwards, indulge in some retail therapy in the various shops and boutiques on Robson Street. Satisfy a sweet tooth at one of the many chocolate shops. End your day with a fabulous dinner at Gotham Steakhouse (see p81). Treat yourself to the best steak in the city, while appreciating the Art Deco heritage surroundings.

See map on pp74–5

Shopping

 1 Roots Canada
MAP J3 ■ 1001 Robson St
■ 604 683 4305

Come here for Canadian-designed sportswear and leatherwear, including a wide range of classic accessories, from watches to belts and backpacks.

2 lululemon athletica
MAP J3 ■ 970 Robson St
■ 604 681 3118

Wildly popular among millennials, this Vancouver-based company sells yoga apparel, athletic gear, and casual wear.

 3 Bute Street Liquor Store
MAP J3 ■ 1155 Bute St
■ 604 660 4569

This large BC Liquor Store carries an extensive variety of well-displayed local BC wines, spirits, beers, and ice wine, made from frozen grapes.

4 RendezVous Art Gallery
MAP K3 ■ 323 Howe St
■ 604 687 7466

The contemporary and traditional Canadian paintings and sculptures at this gallery reflect West Coast beauty. First Nations and Inuit artists are well represented.

5 Herschel Supply Co.
MAP J3 ■ 1080 Robson St
■ www.herschelsupplyco.co.uk

Born in Vancouver, this accessories brand is known for minimalist bags and hats. For locals, a Herschel toque is a year-round fashion staple.

 6 Holt Renfrew
MAP K3 ■ 737 Dunsmuir St
■ 604 681 3121

Dating back to the early 1800s, this is a uniquely Canadian brand. The iconic Vancouver luxury fashion department store offers in-store boutiques, including Louis Vuitton and Chanel.

7 Aritzia
MAP K4 ■ 1100 Robson St
■ 604 684 3251

The haunt of trendy Vancouverites, Aritzia is a homegrown store selling stylish clothing and accessories.

 8 MAC Cosmetics
MAP J3 ■ 908 Robson St
■ 604 682 6588

A Canadian original, this is one of the world's leading cosmetic manufacturers known for its wide range.

9 Murchie's Tea & Coffee
MAP K3 ■ 815 W Hastings St
■ 604 669 0783

The Murchie family began selecting and selling fair-trade tea and coffee on the West Coast in 1894 and the tradition continues today.

 10 John Fluevog Shoes
MAP K4 ■ 837 Granville St
■ 604 688 2828

Fluevog's funky, trendy, yet sturdy shoes and boots are always being snapped up by the fashion savvy.

Interior of John Fluevog Shoes

Bars and Clubs

A Sleater-Kinney show at Commodore Ballroom

1 Commodore Ballroom
MAP K4 ▪ 868 Granville St
▪ 604 739 4550

A Vancouver institution since 1929, this club (see p57) hosts popular tick-eted rock, pop, blues, and jazz acts.

2 Reflections: The Garden Terrace
MAP J4 ▪ 801 W Georgia St
▪ 604 673 7043

Nibble on tapas and sip creative cocktails at this rooftop bar and lounge at the Rosewood Hotel Georgia.

3 Botanist
MAP L3 ▪ 1038 Canada Pl
▪ 604 695 5500

A contemporary spot (see p56) for trying fine wines and cocktails with a Pacific Northwest spin.

4 Library Square Public House
MAP K4 ▪ 300 W Georgia St
▪ 604 633 9644

Enjoy the well-curated range of craft beers on tap at this lively sports pub.

5 Lift Bar & Grill
MAP J2 ▪ 333 Menchion Mews
▪ 604 689 5438

Taste the excellent whiskey and wine at this sophisticated waterfront bar (see p56) with views of Coal Harbour.

6 Six Acres
MAP K4 ▪ 203 Carrall St
▪ 604 488 0110

An inviting gastropub, located inside a lovely brick building.

7 UVA Wine & Cocktail Bar
MAP K4 ▪ 900 Seymour St ▪ 604 632 9560

Operating as a café by day and a snazzy lounge by night, UVA offers tapas and seasonal cocktails. Live music on weekends.

8 One Under
MAP L3 ▪ 476 Granville St ▪ 604 559 4653

Come prepared to practice your swing at this laid-back basement watering hole and pizza restaurant. The six golf simulation bays here promise an entertaining night out.

One Under's relaxed seating area

9 The Roxy
MAP K4 ▪ 932 Granville St
▪ 604 331 7999

This pulsating nightclub (see p57) is where Vancouverites go to dance to local and Canadian bands. Arrive early during the weekends, as the crowd tends to increase steadily.

10 JOEY Burrard
MAP J4 ▪ 820 Burrard St
▪ 604 683 5639

A branch of the industrial-style and lively homegrown bar and restaurant chain, JOEY serves great local wines and has consis-tently good service. Try one of the ice-blended peach Bellini cocktails.

See map on pp74–5

Live Music Venues

1 Queen Elizabeth Theatre
MAP L4 ▪ 630 Hamilton St
▪ www.queenelizabeththeatre.org

This popular theatre hosts Broadway shows and big music acts such as Ed Sheeran and Bonnie Raitt.

Queen Elizabeth theatre in Hamilton St

2 Ventura Room
MAP L4 ▪ 695 Cambie St
▪ 604 620 5547

This bar has vintage-style decor and an outdoor patio. There is live music here every night performed by local and national bands.

3 Oceans 999
MAP L2 ▪ Pan Pacific Vancouver, 300–999 Canada Pl ▪ 604 895 2480

Enjoy an extravagant Italian Opera Buffet while admiring pretty ocean vistas every Saturday night at this spot located in the Pan Pacific hotel.

4 Live Bait Marine Pub
MAP J2 ▪ 1583 Coal Harbour Quay ▪ 604 669 7666

Tucked away inside the marina-side Cardero's Restaurant, this cozy spot has local talent stringing their guitars Sunday through Thursday after 9pm.

5 The Vogue Theatre
MAP K4 ▪ 918 Granville St
▪ 604 688 1975

A nod to the Granville strip's history as Theatre Row, The Vogue has a

1940s-era feel. It's the place to see top music gigs of all genres and performing arts from around the world.

6 Frankie's Jazz Club
MAP L4 ▪ 755 Beatty St
▪ 604 688 6368

Sip on a glass of BC wine, and enjoy exquisite Italian fare paired with fantastic live jazz at this venue every night, Thursday through Sunday. Both local as well as international jazz musicians are proudly featured.

7 Railway Stage & Beer Café
MAP K3 ▪ 579 Dunsmuir St
▪ 604 564 1430

Established in the 1930s, this café hosts local and traveling bands, plus a set of interesting comedy acts nightly. The expansive menu of craft beers is an added delight.

8 The Orpheum
MAP K4 ▪ 601 Smithe St
▪ 604 665 3035

Known as the home of the Vancouver Symphony Orchestra, this lavish venue also hosts local and international choirs and other musical acts.

9 Calabash Bistro
MAP M4 ▪ 428 Carrall St
▪ 604 568 5882 ▪ Closed Mon

Bands playing reggae, blues, and funk generate a fun vibe in the downstairs lounge on most nights, while the dining room upstairs offers a selection of delicious and colorful Caribbean fare.

10 Trees Organic
MAP L3 ▪ 450 Granville St
▪ 604 684 5022

This quaint café (known for its amazing selection of cheesecake) hosts an all ages open mic night on Thursdays and live music on Fridays.

Restaurants

1 Gotham Steakhouse
MAP K3 ■ 615 Seymour St
■ 604 605 8282 ■ $$$

Indulge in the seafood tower filled with fresh crab, prawns, and oysters, or choose from the choicest steaks. End your meal with the bourbon cake.

2 Ancora
MAP K4 ■ 1600 Howe St ■ $$$

The seafood-focused meals here thoughtfully blend Peruvian flavors with Japanese and West Coast cuisines. The interior is bright and stylish.

3 Forage
MAP J3 ■ 1300 Robson St ■ 604 661 1400 ■ $$

Set in the Listel Hotel (see p116), this gathering spot (see p59) for locavores is all about sustainable dining and organic produce.

Paella brunch at Medina Café

4 Diva at the Met
MAP K3
■ Metropolitan Hotel, 645 Howe St ■ 604 602 7788 ■ $$$

In the open kitchen (see p59), chefs conjure up gastronomical magic. An exceptional wine list offers BC wines.

5 Nightingale
MAP K3 ■ 1017 W Hastings St
■ 604 695 9500 ■ $$

Owned by local celebrity chef David Hawksworth, this laid-back yet refined spot serves modern Canadian cuisine.

6 Coast
MAP J3 ■ 1054 Alberni St
■ 604 685 5010 ■ $$

This vibrant place showcases BC's finest, freshest fish and seafood. Be sure to try one of the seafood towers.

7 Le Crocodile
MAP J3 ■ 100-909 Burrard St
■ 604 669 4298 ■ $$$

Alsatian tart has been the signature dish at this elegant French restaurant

PRICE CATEGORIES
For a three-course meal for one with half a bottle of wine (or equivalent meal), taxes, and extra charges.
....
$ under $35 $$ $35–85 $$$ over $85

for many years. The list of French wines here is extensive, and the service is impeccable.

8 Medina Café
MAP K4 ■ 780 Richards St
■ 604 879 3114 ■ Closed D ■ $$

One of the best brunch spots in the city, this unique café serves strong coffee and potent cocktails along with Mediterranean-style food – cassoulet, paella, and couscous.

9 Hawksworth
MAP K3 ■ 801 W Georgia St ■ 604 673 7000 ■ $$$

Contemporary cuisine is the order of the day at this restaurant (see p59) set in the glamorous Rosewood Hotel Georgia (see p116).

10 CinCin Ristorante & Bar
MAP J3 ■ 1154 Robson St
■ 604 688 7338 ■ Closed L ■ $$$

Delicious rotisserie meats, risotto, and pasta are served in this Italian-themed restaurant (see p59) popular with visiting Hollywood stars.

Terrace at CinCin Ristorante & Bar

See map on pp74–5 ←

🔟 South Granville, Kitsilano, and Yaletown

The picturesque Granville Bridge and False Creek separate the neighborhoods of South Granville and Yaletown. On the south shore, South Granville offers a pleasant mix of ritzy shops and restaurants. Granville Island is a bustling maze of converted warehouses, with a large public market as its centerpiece. Nearby, the hip Kitsilano area is home to a host of cultural attractions. Yaletown, on the north shore of False Creek, which began life as a railway works yard now booms with condos, boutiques, bars, and eateries.

Ship figurehead in the Vancouver Maritime Museum

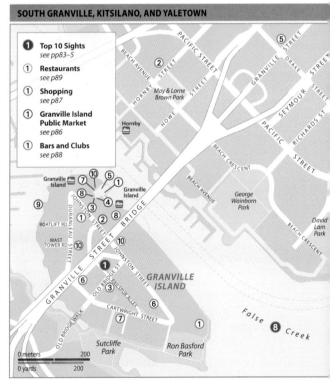

SOUTH GRANVILLE, KITSILANO, AND YALETOWN

- **① Top 10 Sights**
  see pp83–5
- **① Restaurants**
  see p89
- **① Shopping**
  see p87
- **① Granville Island Public Market**
  see p86
- **① Bars and Clubs**
  see p88

Fishermen's Wharf, Granville Island

1 Granville Island

The original mudflats of False Creek were a fishing ground for the Squamish people. Industry moved in, polluting much of the turn-of-the-19th-century city. In the 1970s, that all changed with the redevelopment of Granville Island (see pp24–5). Under the aegis of the federal government, heavy industry moved out and Granville Island quickly became a colorful, lively, bustling community.

2 Sunset Beach
MAP H4

The white sands of Sunset Beach (see p47), which marks the end of English Bay and the start of False Creek, provide an ideal setting for swimming. In summer, water temperatures rise to 65° F (18° C), and lifeguards are on duty from mid-May to Labour Day. The west end of Sunset Beach provides a good view of the granite Inukshuk (see p43). The Vancouver Aquatic Centre, at the east end of the beach, has an Olympic-size swimming pool. False Creek Ferries (see p111) dock behind the center.

Street in Yaletown Warehouse District

3 Yaletown Warehouse District
MAP J4–K5

Several warehouses here have been transformed into lofts and stores, café terraces have sprung up on old loading docks, and high-rises have filled Yaletown's skyline. Along with the new residents has come a face-lift. Homer, Hamilton, and Mainland streets have been tastefully spruced up, making the most of heritage architectural features, including the red brick and arched doorways. Many brew pubs and nightclubs keep the area hopping at night.

4 Vancouver Maritime Museum

MAP G4 ▪ 1905 Ogden Ave ▪ 604 257 8300 ▪ Open 10am–5pm Tue–Sun ▪ Adm ▪ www.vanmaritime.com

Highlights of the West Coast's rich maritime history include seagoing canoes and a 1928 RCMP schooner, which was the first ship to circumnavigate North America. Kids can play with the discovery center's *(see p41)* telescopes and underwater robot.

5 H. R. MacMillan Space Centre

MAP G4 ▪ 1100 Chestnut St ▪ 604 738 7827 ▪ Open 9:30am–4:30pm daily (to 11:30pm Wed & Fri) ▪ Adm

Space lore is presented in hands-on displays and multimedia shows here. A demonstration theater and the Cosmic Courtyard's interactive gallery bring space to life. The Planetarium's multimedia shows feature space and astronomy inside a 65-ft (20-m) dome.

6 Roundhouse Community Arts & Recreation Centre

MAP K5 ▪ 181 Roundhouse Mews ▪ 604 713 1800 ▪ www.roundhouse.ca

Located off Pacific Boulevard, inside a former Canadian Pacific Railway switching building, the Roundhouse includes theater and gallery spaces and a host of community arts and athletic programs. Also housed in this centre is the locomotive that pulled the first passenger train to Vancouver in 1887.

Locomotive 374 in the Roundhouse

7 Gallery Row

MAP H6 ▪ 2100-2400 Granville St

Nearly a dozen commercial art and antique galleries line the four-block stretch of Granville Street between 5th Avenue and West Broadway.

Vanier Park, with Downtown Vancouver rising behind

Art forms ranging from sculpture to photography and paintings are all well represented at this unique spot.

False Creek
MAP J6–L5

As its name implies, False Creek isn't a creek at all but a saltwater inlet. It extends east from Burrard Bridge to Science World. In the 1850s, Captain G. H. Richards sailed up this body of water, eastward to Clark Drive, hoping to find the Fraser River. Disappointed, he named it False Creek. The mudflats he saw were fishing grounds for the Squamish people. Today, paved False Creek Seawall joins English Bay Seawall east of Burrard Bridge and circles the creek. It's ideal for joggers, cyclists, and walkers.

⑨ Museum of Vancouver
MAP G5 ▪ **1100 Chestnut St** ▪ **604 736 4431** ▪ **Open 10am–5pm Sun–Wed (to 8pm Thu–Sat)** ▪ **Adm**

Canada's largest civic museum hosts exhibits ranging from a fur-trading post to an amazing display of neon signs. Artifacts from a huge collection make up natural history, archaeology, Asian arts, and ethnology displays.

⑩ Vanier Park
MAP G4

This park is a calming oasis. Boats sail by on English Bay, and pedestrians pass through on route to Kitsilano Beach or Granville Island. Coast Salish people once inhabited the park area. It is now home to the H. R. MacMillan Space Centre, Museum of Vancouver, and Vancouver Maritime Museum.

A DAY IN YALETOWN, GRANVILLE ISLAND, AND KITSILANO

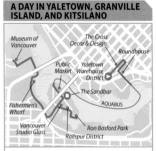

▶ MORNING

Start in **Yaletown Warehouse District** (see p83) at the corner of Drake and Hamilton streets for a 15-minute stroll north on Hamilton, noting its historic buildings. At Helmcken Street, turn right, then right again at Mainland Street. Spend half an hour in the shops, ending at **The Cross Decor & Design** (see p87). Cross Pacific Boulevard to admire the **Roundhouse**'s locomotive 374. Take 15 minutes to explore the complex, then hop on the **Aquabus** (see p111) from the dock behind the center for the trip to **Granville Island** (see p83). For a fun hour, wander the **Public Market** (see p86), buying food for a casual lunch on a waterside bench.

AFTERNOON

Exit the market's east side, and continue on Johnston Street past Ocean Concrete. Turn right on Old Bridge Street to watch the glassblowers at **Vancouver Studio Glass** (see p24). Walk to **Railspur District** (see p25), on your left. Browse the shops for about 20 minutes, then cross Railspur Park to Cartwright Street. Turn left and walk to the end, to Ron Basford Park, where kids love running up "the mound." Back on Johnston Street, head west walking along the Seawall, passing by **Fishermen's Wharf** toward Vanier Park to find the large **Museum of Vancouver**, allowing yourself an hour there. End the day at **The Sandbar** (see p89) for breathtaking views of the market, False Creek, and the city's West End.

See map on pp82–3 ⟵

Granville Island Public Market

 International Food Courts
Two food courts offer sit-down and takeout food, including Japanese, Thai, Mexican, and Greek. Patience may be required to land one of the limited indoor tables.

 Stuart's Bakery
Mouthwatering pies, chocolate confections, and pastries fill one counter; multigrain, cheese, and other loaves crowd the other.

Fruit tart from Stuart's Bakery

 JJ Bean
The Granville Island outlet was JJ Bean's very first coffee shop, which opened next to their roastery. The roast is full bodied and rich and all drinks are takeout – you can buy beans but there are no baked goods.

 Olde World Fudge
Irresistible Belgian chocolate treats are concocted on-site in a copper vat. Assorted gift boxes include fudge, toffee, brittles, and caramel apples. Samples available.

5 Public Market Courtyard
On the east side of the market, enjoy tucking into your food as you take in the free entertainment in the open-air waterside Market Courtyard. The courtyard's worn floor planks from its days as an industrial dock only add to the charm.

6 Day Vendors
Specialty stalls sell an assortment of locally made wares, including seasonal and one-off items. Bowls made of BC wood, Thai curry sauces, herb seedlings, homemade pies, and jewelry are just the start. Vendors may not be located in the same place from day to day.

7 Granville Island Market Tour
Foodie Tours: 604 295 8844; www.foodietours.ca
If you're keen to get tastings from artisans across the market, sign up for a foodie market tour. The knowledgeable guides lead you to the very best local producers and you'll try cured meats, cheeses, donuts, and fruit, among other delectable delights.

8 Lee's Donuts
Hailed as one of the best donut makers on the West Coast, this Granville Island institution (it's been here since 1979) serves the lightest, fluffiest donuts you will ever taste, and you can watch them being made.

9 Marina
At the marina on the market's west side you'll find fancy yachts, sail boats, and the occasional fishing boat. Tall ships dock here during festivals.

10 Public Market Building
At Granville Island's west end is the large Public Market, partly housed inside a wood-frame, corrugated tin-clad warehouse. Constructed in the early 1920s by the Island's first tenant, BC Equipment, this structure set the architectural style of the Island. Its timbered beams and massive pulleys and hooks once pulled rope coils from one area to the other.

Exterior of the Public Market Building

Shopping

Wood crafts at the Circle Craft Co-op

1 Circle Craft Co-op
MAP H5 ■ 1666 Johnston St
■ 604 669 8021

The best of BC crafts, from handmade clothing to one-of-a-kind jewelry. There's also wall art, wood crafts ceramics, and hand-blown glass.

2 Meinhardt Fine Foods
MAP B2 ■ 3002 Granville St
■ 604 732 4405

With a design similar to New York City's famous store Dean & DeLuca, this iconic food emporium in South Granville stocks fresh ingredients that are replenished regularly.

3 The Cross Decor & Design
MAP J5 ■ 1198 Homer St ■ 604 689 2900

Located in a 1914 heritage building, this home decor store sources items from all over the world, and also sells pieces by local artists and vendors.

4 Bacci's
MAP B2 ■ 2788 Granville St
■ 604 733 4933

This boutique is known for its unique and high-end women's clothing, housewares, and bath products.

5 Wildlife Thrift Store
MAP K3 ■ 1295 Granville St
■ 604 682 0381

Browse for treasures at this compact thrift shop, stocked with books, shoes, clothes, and vintage kitchenware.

6 Opus Art Supplies
MAP H6 ■ 1360 Johnston St
■ 604 736 7028

This iconic Granville Island art shop is stocked with everything an artist needs. Fine art workshops are often held here too.

7 Forge and Form
MAP H6 ■ 1334 Cartwright St
■ 604 684 6298

High-end gold and silver jewelry with precious stones. Choose from bold rings and pretty, fluid necklaces.

8 Swirl Wine Store
MAP K5 ■ 1185 Mainland St
■ 604 408 9463

Grab the best selection of BC wines at vineyard prices, as well as gourmet gift baskets at this delightful store. It also offers free wine-tasting sessions.

Tasting at Swirl Wine Store

9 Boboli
MAP B2 ■ 2776 Granville St
■ 604 257 2300

Trend-setting styles from a variety of lines, including Missoni, Canada Goose, and Arc'teryx Veilance.

10 Malaspina Printmakers Gallery
MAP H5 ■ 1555 Duranleau St
■ 604 688 1724

Prints by Canadian (particularly BC) and international artists with images and styles to suit all tastes.

See map on pp82–3

Bars and Clubs

Dockside Restaurant and Brewing Company

1 Dockside Restaurant and Brewing Company

This popular bar is located in the Granville Island Hotel (see p117). Savor the delicious beer brewed here while admiring the boats on False Creek from the fantastic patio area.

2 Long Table Distillery
MAP K3 ■ 1451 Hornby St ■ 604 266 0177 ■ Closed Sun–Tue

This is the first micro-distillery of the city, crafting small-batch gin and premium spirits. Enjoy the light snacks and cocktails on weekends.

3 The Liberty Distillery
MAP H5 ■ 1494 Old Bridge St ■ 604 558 1998

Only BC-grown grains and ingredients go into the spirits here, which are fermented and distilled on-site in handmade copper stills. Book a tour or pop into the lounge for a cocktail.

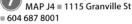

Cocktail at the Liberty Distillery

4 Yaletown Brewing Company
MAP K5 ■ 1111 Mainland St ■ 604 681 2739

Choose from the extensive selection of locally brewed beer here while dining on some excellent homestyle cooking in the pub, the restaurant, or out on the popular patio.

5 Hello Goodbye Bar
MAP K5 ■ 1120 Hamilton St. ■ Open Thu–Sat ■ 604 699 6292

Visitors enter this speakeasy-style bar through an unmarked basement door. Expect cocktails and DJs spinning late into the night.

6 Granville Island Brewing
Established in 1984, the brewery (see pp24–5) is the place to buy bottles, get your growler refilled, or reserve a keg for an event. It organizes tours and tastings, but you'll get a warm welcome in the industrial-feel taproom too.

7 The Refinery
MAP J4 ■ 1115 Granville St ■ 604 687 8001

Modern and eco-conscious wine and cocktail bar known for its inventive drinks and Latin-inspired tapas made with locally sourced ingredients.

8 Backstage Lounge
MAP H5 ■ 1585 Johnston St ■ 604 687 1354

This low-key hangout attracts theatergoers and actors from the Granville Island Stage next door. Live music is performed, with a focus on local talent.

9 Grapes & Soda
MAP H6 ■ 1541 W 6th Ave ■ 604 336 2456

Cozy wine bar serving organic wines, cocktails, and farm-to-table small bites, plus local charcuterie.

10 Bar None
MAP J5 ■ 1222 Hamilton St ■ 604 689 7000 ■ Closed Sun–Thu

In a converted warehouse, this New York-style nightclub has live music, a dance floor, and ample seating.

Restaurants

1 **Blue Water Café**
MAP K4 ■ 1095 Hamilton St ■ 604 688 8078 ■ Closed L ■ $$$

On offer here (see p58) are masterfully prepared West Coast dishes cooked with the freshest local fish, most of which is sustainably sourced.

2 **Rodney's Oyster House**
MAP J5 ■ 1228 Hamilton St ■ 604 609 0080 ■ $$

The action is at the counter, so sidle up and order any of the many oyster types on offer, shucked as you watch. Steamed clams and mussels, crab, and Atlantic lobster are also featured.

3 **Cioppino's Mediterranean Grill**
MAP J5 ■ 1133 Hamilton St ■ 604 688 7466 ■ Closed Sun & Mon ■ $$$

Chef "Pino" Posteraro creates lighter versions of traditional Italian pasta, risottos, and seafood (see p59).

4 **Salmon n' Bannock Bistro**
MAP B2 ■ 7–1128 W Broadway ■ 604 568 8971 ■ $$

A First Nations-owned bistro serving seasonal and traditional Indigenous meals, including bannock fry bread, pemmican, and bison roast.

Well-lit entrance to The Sandbar

5 **Provence Marinaside**
MAP K5 ■ 1177 Marinaside Cres ■ 604 681 4144 ■ $$

This pretty restaurant and bar has a sommelier to help select wine, and picnic baskets are available, too.

6 **The Flying Pig**
MAP J5 ■ 1168 Hamilton St ■ 604 568 1344 ■ $$

With a casual setting, this restaurant serves innovative Canadian cuisine. Try the classic poutine with pulled pork.

7 **Small Victory Bakery**
MAP K4 ■ 1088 Homer St ■ 604 899 8892 ■ Closed D ■ $

A modern café that offers wonderful croissants and cakes, as well as light breakfast and lunch snacks.

8 **Brix & Mortar**
MAP K5 ■ 1137 Hamilton St ■ 604 915 9463 ■ Closed L & Mon ■ $$

Set in a 1912 heritage building, this wine and tapas bar has excellent set menus featuring West Coast cuisine.

9 **Beaucoup Bakery**
MAP H6 ■ 2150 Fir St ■ 604 732 4222 ■ $

Locals line up early for the pretty pastries here, both traditional and unusual. Vancouver's 49th Parallel Coffee Roasters' coffee is served too.

10 **The Sandbar**
MAP H5 ■ 1535 Johnston St ■ 604 669 9030 ■ $$

Feast on Dungeness crab cakes and cedar-planked salmon while enjoying breathtaking views of False Creek.

TOP 10 Vancouver Island

A world away from buzzing Vancouver, but easily accessible by ferry or seaplane, picturesque Vancouver Island is where city folk go for

downtime. Located at the very south of the island, the provincial capital Victoria is the first stop for most visitors. The rest of the sparsely populated island offers protected parkland, endless beaches, offshore islets, and fishing villages.

Black bear in Clayoquot Sound

① Clayoquot Sound
MAP A4

Pronounced "cla-kwat," Clayoquot hosts 1,700-year-old trees. Tofino (see p33), Ucluelet (see p32), and several First Nations communities share the UNESCO biosphere reserve with black bears, elk, cougars, wolves, and an endangered bird, the marbled murrelet. The coastline has scenic bays, intertidal lagoons, and mudflats.

VANCOUVER ISLAND

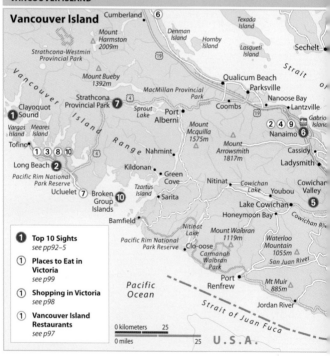

Vancouver Island

①	Top 10 Sights	see pp92–5
①	Places to Eat in Victoria	see p99
①	Shopping in Victoria	see p98
①	Vancouver Island Restaurants	see p97

0 kilometers 25
0 miles 25

Previous pages Sunset over Georgia Strait from a beach in Nanaimo

Shoreline of Long Beach after a sunset, Pacific Rim National Park

② Long Beach

The 16-km (10-mile) stretch of coastline (see pp32–3) located between Tofino (see p33) and Ucluelet (see p32) is a part of the Pacific Rim National Park Reserve. Backed by forests and with wide vistas of the wild Pacific Ocean, it is a must-see. Visitors can hike, surf, and also learn about the Nuu-chah-nulth peoples, who have inhabited this region for centuries.

③ Gulf Islands
MAP E5

Many visitors flock to these islands in the Strait of Georgia. Salt Spring, with its many artists' studios, and Galiano, which has a lovely provincial park, are the most popular island destinations. Saturna, Pender, Mayne, and Gabriola are the other major islands. Each has its own personality; all are accessible by ferry (see p110) from Swartz Bay.

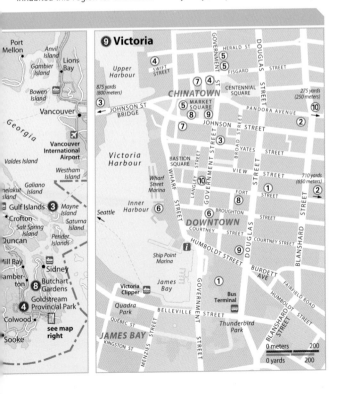

Stream at Goldstream Provincial Park

4 Goldstream Provincial Park

MAP E6 ▪ Visitor Centre: 2930 Trans Canada Hwy ▪ 250 478 9414 ▪ Open 9am–4:30pm daily

Massive old-growth Douglas firs tower overhead in this mystic rain forest only 12 miles (19 km) from Victoria. The park's waterfall drops 155 ft (48 m) into a canyon pool and is easily accessible by foot. An annual salmon run on the Goldstream River during fall attracts hundreds of majestic bald eagles. Once a fishing ground for the Coast Salish, the park was overrun by miners during the Gold Rush of the 1850s (see p38). A visitor centre provides information on the park.

5 Cowichan Valley
MAP D5

This pastoral valley is a mix of forests as well as farmland. Its wines, ciders, and gourmet cheeses attract foodies from miles around. Cowichan Lake is Vancouver Island's main freshwater lake and a terrific spot for swimming, canoeing, and fishing. The Cowichan River is also famed for its fly-fishing.

DUNCAN, THE CITY OF TOTEMS

The world's largest outdoor collection of totem poles can be explored in Duncan, a city on the traditional lands of the Cowichan First Nation in the Cowichan Valley. Carved in western red cedar, the totem designs represent family crests and traditional symbols in Coast Salish and Kwakwaka'wakw culture, and were once a record of significant events.

---

6 Nanaimo

MAP D4 ▪ The Bastion: 98 Front St; open 11am–3:30pm Sat & Sun (summer only) ▪ Nanaimo Museum: 100 Museum Way; open 10am–4pm Tue–Sat; adm; www.nanaimomuseum.ca

The Old Quarter, built when Nanaimo was a coal-mining town, boasts many 19th-century buildings, including the 1895 Nanaimo Court House. Pay a visit to The Bastion Nanaimo Museum at the Harbourfront Walkway. From the seaside, you can see Protection and Newcastle Islands.

7 Strathcona Provincial Park

www.bcparks.ca

The vast area of mountain wilderness in the interior of Vancouver Island has been a provincial park since 1911. Snowy peaks make a stunning backdrop to the park's many hiking trails; at 7,218 ft (2,200 m) the Golden Hinde dominates the southern region of the island. Buttle Lake is a popular place to set up camp.

8 Butchart Gardens

MAP E5 ▪ 800 Benvenuto Ave, Brentwood Bay ▪ 250 652 4422 ▪ Open daily ▪ Adm ▪ www.butchartgardens.com

For over a century, the incomparable Butchart Gardens (see p48), wrung out of a worked-out quarry, have awed visitors with their lush beauty.

Sunken garden at Butchart Gardens

9 Victoria

With many outstanding historic and cultural sights, including the Royal BC Museum, artist Emily Carr's House, and the Art Gallery of Greater Victoria, the provincial capital *(see pp28–9)* makes a pleasant base for visits to Vancouver Island. A mild climate, lovely parks and gardens, and great vistas from the Inner Harbour add to the city's charm. The waters around Victoria are also a great spot for whale-watching, especially between May and November.

Sea kayaking around Barkley Sound

10 Broken Group Islands
MAP B5

An archipelago of some 100 rugged islands and islets is a paradise for nature lovers, kayakers, and scuba divers. The area around Barkley Sound has outstanding views of coastal rain forest, beaches, and sea caves. Accessible only by boat, this isolated wilderness is best experienced via a guided tour.

WALKING TOUR OF VICTORIA

▶ MORNING

Starting at the corner of Humboldt Street and Douglas Street visit the **Maritime Museum of British Columbia** *(see p29)* and devote an hour to its displays before heading north on Government Street. At Fisgard Street, the Chinese-style Gate of Harmonious Interest welcomes you to **Chinatown** *(see p29)*. Explore the area for an hour, dipping into tiny Fan Tan Alley, off Fisgard Street. Continue south to Bastion Square, the heart of Old Town, where fur traders boozed and brawled in the days of Fort Victoria. Head to the **Irish Times Pub** *(1200 Government St; open 8–1am daily)* for fish and chips.

AFTERNOON

Pause to admire the marine traffic from the **Inner Harbour** *(see p28)*. At the far end of the harbor, cross Belleville Street to view the Queen Victoria statue by the **BC Parliament Buildings** *(see pp28–9)*. The fascinating **Royal BC Museum** *(see pp28–9)* next door will take about two hours to peruse. Exit the museum on the east side to admire the fascinating totem poles in **Thunderbird Park** *(see p30)* before checking out the historic **Helmcken House** *(see p31)* nearby. Cross Belleville Street to the **Fairmont Empress Hotel** *(see p119)* for a glimpse of the grand lobby. Have dinner at **Red Fish Blue Fish** *(see p99)* located by the waterfront on Broughton Street Pier to replenish your energy.

See map on pp92–3 ←

Outdoor Activities

1 Rock Climbing

Strathcona Park Lodge: 41040 Gold River Hwy, Campbell River, 250 286 3122; www.strathconapark lodge.com
Climbers can explore any one of the three bluffs and view the vistas across Upper Campbell Lake, with the guided tours of Strathcona Park Lodge.

2 Fishing

Both fly-fishing and salmon fishing are popular. The action-packed east coast Campbell River, known as "the salmon capital of the world," is a highlight February through to March.

3 Hiking
In summer, hikers gravitate to the West Coast Trail (see p33). Just as picturesque, but shorter, are the Juan de Fuca Marine Trail, the Rainforest Trail, and Wild Pacific Trail.

4 Skiing

Mount Washington Alpine Resort: www.mountwashington.ca
Mount Washington has some of the best powder in BC to ski, snowboard, cross-country, and toboggan.

5 Camping
Scenic campgrounds are scattered across Vancouver Island and the Gulf Islands. Hello BC (see p115) and the BC tourism website have comprehensive listings.

Kayaking in the Strait of Georgia

6 Kayaking and Canoeing

Ocean River Sports: 250 381 4233; www.oceanriver.com
For ocean paddling there's the Broken Group Islands, Clayoquot Sound, the Gulf Islands, and Nanaimo. If you like lakes, explore Elk and Beaver Lake. Hire equipment at Ocean River Sports.

7 Diving
Sink or Swim Scuba: 250 758 7946; www.scubananaimo.ca
Winter diving is best for visibility. Popular dive spots include Barkley Sound, Browning Wall, Discovery, and wrecks off the coast close to Nanaimo. Sink or Swim Scuba offers equipment hire and PADI courses.

8 Biking
From gentle cycling in Victoria to serious off-road mountain biking in the Comox Valley, Vancouver Island has something for everyone. For bikepackers, the 620-mile (1,000-km) Tree to Sea Loop is phenomenal.

9 Surfing
Pacific Surf School: 250 725 2155
■ Surf Sister Surf School: 250 725 4456
Access to the wild West Coast and the Pacific Ocean make surfing popular on Vancouver Island, especially in Tofino and Long Beach. Chesterman Beach is a great place for beginners.

10 Whale-Watching
Between April and October, you can spot resident orcas (killer whales). In May, June, September and October, migratory humpback whales pass the BC coast, and gray whales (see p32) do so in spring. You can see minke whales all year round.

Scenic camping in the snow

Vancouver Island Restaurants

1 Shelter
634 Campbell St, Tofino
▪ 250 725 3353 ▪ $$

A charming nautical-inspired spot perched above the marina. It has a locally-sourced menu that includes fresh seafood and burgers.

2 Nori Japanese Restaurant
6750 Island Hwy, Unit 203, Nanaimo
▪ 250 751 3377 ▪ $

The location of this award-winning restaurant might not inspire (it's set on the highway), but the sushi and sashimi are the best in town.

Dinner with a view at the Pointe Restaurant

3 The Pointe Restaurant
Wickaninnish Inn, 500 Osprey Ln, Tofino ▪ 250 725 3106 ▪ $$$

Offering panoramic views of the wild Pacific Ocean, this restaurant has a great fine-dining menu. Try the weekly tasting menu paired with BC wines.

4 Bee's Knees Café
3200 Island Hwy N, Nanaimo
▪ 250 591 5250 ▪ Closed D ▪ $

This cozy community café has a limited menu, which changes daily, but the great coffee is a staple.

5 Yayu
250 Main St, Ucluelet
▪ Open Wed–Sun ▪ Closed D
▪ www.yayucafe.com ▪ $

A vegan café known for its use of local, natural and nutrient-packed ingredients.

PRICE CATEGORIES
For a three-course meal for one with half a bottle of wine (or equivalent meal), taxes, and extra charges.
....
$ under $35 $$ $35–85 $$$ over $85

---

6 Blackfin Pub
132 Port Augusta St, Comox
▪ 250 339 5030 ▪ $$

Blackfin is an inviting, marina-facing pub with a large patio for dining in the summer, and seating by the fireplace in winter. Try the stuffed beef Yorkshire, the fish and chips, or the oyster burger.

7 Pluvio
1714 Peninsula Rd, Ucluelet ▪ 250 726 7001 ▪ $$$

This fine-dining place with an outdoor terrace is known for its wine-bar feel. There are plenty of seafood options and everything is seasonal and cooked to perfection.

8 Common Loaf
180 First St, Tofino
▪ 250 725 3915 ▪ Closed D ▪ $

An institution in Tofino, this quirky cash-only bakeshop has provided the town with artisan breads and sweet baked goods for years.

9 Gabriel's Gourmet Café
39A Commercial St, Nanaimo
▪ 250 714 0271 ▪ $

Set right in the heart of Nanaimo is Gabriel's, where locally sourced ingredients are a mainstay of the bistro fare. Brunch is served until 3pm.

10 Chocolate Tofino
1180 A Pacific Rim Hwy, Tofino
▪ 250 725 2526 ▪ $

Exquisite handcrafted chocolate, gelato and sorbet are served in this tiny shack – you can even watch the chocolatiers at work. There are long lines for the tasty gelato in summer.

See map on pp92–3

Shopping in Victoria

Items for sale in Fort Street Antiques

1 Fort Street Antiques
MAP Q3 ▪ Fort St between Douglas St & Cook St

Discover one-of-a-kind silverware, glass and china, fine art, furniture, and jewelry on upper Fort Street.

2 WIN Pandora
MAP Q2 ▪ 785 Pandora Ave ▪ 250 480 4006

Victoria's community cooperative Women In Need (WIN) has several secondhand boutiques dotted around the city; Pandora is a great place to find vintage clothing and accessories.

3 Bernstein & Gold
MAP P2 ▪ 608 Yates St ▪ 250 384 7899

Head to this lifestyle boutique for carefully chosen homewares, jewelry, footwear, leather goods, as well as great skin-care brands and a mini spa.

4 Silk Road Tea
MAP P1 ▪ 1624 Government St ▪ 250 382 0006

Silk Road offers a tea-tasting bar similar to a wine bar. In addition to tea, it has a spa *(see p44)* and its own line of natural body-care products.

5 Paboom
MAP P2 ▪ 1437 Store St ▪ 250 380 0020

A budget-friendly and modern shop for home decor, Paboom also stocks unique gifts for people of all ages.

6 Rogers' Chocolates
MAP P3 ▪ 913 Government St ▪ 250 881 8771

At this long-established chocolatier, sweets are made with fair trade cocoa. Some selections come in tins.

7 Fan Tan Home & Style
MAP P1 ▪ 523 Fisgard St ▪ 250 382 4424

This store sells gifts from around the world, with a focus on India, Indonesia, China, and France. Home accessories include mats, art, baskets, linens, and curios.

8 Violette Boutique
MAP P2 ▪ 560 Johnson St ▪ 250 388 7752

Inspired by Paris jewelry boutiques, the owner stocks mainly Canadian-made pieces, both dainty and chunky.

9 Mountain Equipment Co-op
MAP P2 ▪ 1450 Government St ▪ 250 386 2667

Canada's best-known outdoors store for adventure gear and clothing.

10 Munro's Books
MAP P2 ▪ 1108 Government St ▪ 250 382 2464

A fantastic bookstore founded by Jim and Alice Munro, the Nobel Prize-winning short story writer.

Exterior of Munro's Books

Places to Eat in Victoria

 Fairmont Empress Hotel
A variety of elegant dining venues await at Victoria's grandest hotel *(see p119)*. Especially popular is the formal afternoon tea, served daily since 1908 – advance reservations are required.

PRICE CATEGORIES

For a three-course meal for one with half a bottle of wine (or equivalent meal), taxes, and extra charges.

$ under $35 $$ $35–85 $$$ over $85

Inside the Fairmont Empress Hotel

 Bear & Joey
MAP E6 ▪ 1025 Cook St ▪ 250 590 9193 ▪ Closed D ▪ $
A beautifully designed café with a vegetarian-friendly menu, including fare such as avocado toast, chickpea salad, and organic juices.

3 Spinnakers Gastro Brewpub
MAP E6 ▪ 308 Catherine St, Victoria ▪ 250 386 2739 ▪ $$
Canada's oldest licensed brewpub serves all-natural smoked meats and sausages, perfect companions to the assortment of beers on tap.

4 Craft Beer Market
MAP N1 ▪ 450 Swift St ▪ 250 361 1940 ▪ $$
Local beer and small bites await at this picnic table-lined patio on the scenic Victoria Harbour waterfront.

 Brasserie L'École
MAP P1 ▪ 1715 Government St ▪ 250 475 6260 ▪ Closed L, Sun & Mon ▪ $$$
This place dishes up French bistro classics – lamb shank, mussels, and *frites* – made using local products.

 Red Fish Blue Fish
MAP N3 ▪ 1006 Wharf St ▪ 250 298 6877 ▪ Closed winter ▪ $
Set in a shipping container on the Inner Harbour, this seasonal canteen-style fish restaurant serves sustainable seafood.

 Il Terrazzo Ristorante
MAP P2 ▪ 555 Johnson St ▪ 250 361 0028 ▪ $$
Enjoy fine Northern Italian food in the heated courtyard here. Wood-oven-roasted meats and pizzas, pastas, and seafood arrive with a flourish.

8 Pagliacci's
MAP P3 ▪ 1011 Broad St ▪ 250 386 1662 ▪ $$
Linguine, lasagna, and fettuccine are superb and satisfying at this Italian place. Don't miss the Pag's bread.

9 Noodlebox
MAP P3 ▪ 818 Douglas St ▪ 250 384 1314 ▪ $
Huge portions of noodle and rice dishes come in decorative boxes here, and there are five levels of spiciness to suit every taste.

10 Wildfire Bakery
MAP E6 ▪ 1517 Quadra St, Victoria ▪ 250 381 3473 ▪ $
This family-owned organic bakery and café offers artisan breads, cakes, as well as pastries, with wholesome savories for breakfast and lunch.

See map on pp92–3

🔟 Greater Vancouver and Beyond

One of the reasons Vancouver is often listed as one of the world's best places to live is the wide range of things to do, and the breathtaking scenery in which to do them, just a short drive away from downtown. The ski slopes and golf courses of Whistler are reached after a scenic two-hour drive, ideal for an overnight excursion. Superb rain forests can be enjoyed on the western side of Vancouver's Pacific Spirit Regional Park and in North Vancouver's Capilano Suspension Bridge Park. Towns like Squamish or the Brackendale community provide unforgettable nature walks, hikes, and climbs. Small waterfront towns such as Steveston, a former fishing village, have proudly preserved their local history.

Exhibit at the Museum of Anthropology at UBC

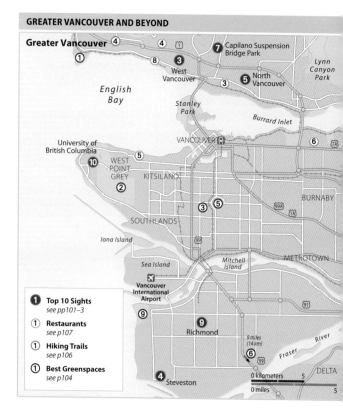

GREATER VANCOUVER AND BEYOND

Greater Vancouver

Capilano Suspension Bridge Park

Lynn Canyon Park

West Vancouver

North Vancouver

English Bay

Stanley Park

Burrard Inlet

University of British Columbia

VANCOUVER

WEST POINT GREY

KITSILANO

BURNABY

SOUTHLANDS

Iona Island

Sea Island

Mitchell Island

METROTOWN

Vancouver International Airport

Richmond

9 miles (14 km)

Fraser River

DELTA

Steveston

0 kilometers 5

0 miles 5

1 Top 10 Sights	see pp101–3
① Restaurants	see p107
① Hiking Trails	see p106
① Best Greenspaces	see p104

Blackcomb Mountain and Harmony Lake in Whistler

1 Whistler

Two mountains, Whistler and Blackcomb, rise side by side at the popular resort town of Whistler (see pp34–5). Ski in winter, enjoy views of the four villages and surrounding mountains and valleys from gondolas and lift chairs year-round, or cycle the Valley Trail in summer.

2 Grouse Mountain

MAP F3 ■ Visitor Centre: 6400 Nancy Greene Way, North Vancouver; 604 980 9311; www.grousemountain. com ■ Adm to Skyride

There's lots to do atop this Vancouver landmark reached via a gondola ride or a steep hike. Enjoy amazing views over the Lower Mainland and beyond, fly on ziplines, learn about local wildlife, or play disc golf. In winter, visitors come here to ski and snowboard.

3 West Vancouver

MAP B1

Horseshoe Bay, Lighthouse Park (see p47) and Cypress Provincial Park (see p104) are among the top scenic attractions in this region. A pleasant day-trip destination, Horseshoe Bay has a small bayside park with two totems. BC Ferries (see p110) depart here for Nanaimo, Bowen Island, and the Sunshine Coast. The pedestrian Centennial Seawall links Ambleside Park and the Dundarave village.

North to Whistler

0 km   15
0 miles   15

1 Whistler
1 9 10
McGuire
6 8 Garibaldi Provincial Park
Garibaldi
Mount Garibaldi 2636m
Ashlu River
BRITISH COLUMBIA
2
8 Brackendale
Garibaldi Highlands
6 Squamish
7
Britannia Beach
99
Pinecone Burke Provincial Park
Pitt River
Indian River
Anvil Island
Gambier Island
1 Brunswick
New Brighton
Lions Bay
Obelisk Peak 1655m
Snug Cove
4 Grouse 2 5 2
9 Mountain 7 7
Bowen Island
10 Coquitlam
VANCOUVER 3
10
see map left
Surrey
8

Point Atkinson Lighthouse in Lighthouse Park

Gulf of Georgia Cannery National Historic Site by the Fraser River, Steveston

4 Steveston
MAP B3 ■ Gulf of Georgia Cannery: 12138 4th Ave; 604 664 9009; open 10am–5pm daily; adm
The old-fashioned Steveston village was built on the salmon industry, with 15 canneries once employing thousands. The Gulf of Georgia Cannery National Historic Site offers a glimpse into this interesting past. The converted 1894 building rests on pylons over the Fraser River. View the film inside, then tour the building. The Ice House has a fun children's discovery area.

5 North Vancouver
MAP B1 ■ Lynn Canyon Park: at the end of Peters Rd, Lynn Valley ■ Lynn Canyon Ecology Centre: 604 990 3755
North Vancouver is a busy North Shore city of more than 53,000 residents. Take the scenic SeaBus ride across Burrard Inlet. Disembark at Lonsdale Quay, a public market selling fresh produce. To the east, Lynn Canyon Park has its own suspension bridge, which spans the dramatic canyon, 165 ft (50 m) above Lynn Creek, as well as nearly 40 types of moss, and 100-year-old Douglas firs. Stop in at the Ecology Centre to view the displays and films, and get details on park tours and trails.

6 Squamish
MAP E3
"Squamish," a Coast Salish word meaning "mother of the wind," is an apt name for this windy town that has become a major center for outdoor activities. Rock climbers relish the challenge of the Stawamus Chief, an imposing granite monolith. Others windsurf on the Squamish River or camp in nearby parks, including the renowned Garibaldi Provincial Park.

Windsurfing in Squamish

A CONVOCATION OF EAGLES

Almost half the world's bald eagle population lives in BC. Thousands make their annual winter home in Brackendale. The first eagle count took place along the Squamish River in 1985, when six people counted 500 eagles. Some 600 to 900 eagles are now counted annually. Brackendale Eagle Festival takes place every January.

7 Capilano Suspension Bridge Park

This North Vancouver park (see pp16–17) was opened in 1888. Its suspension bridge sways 230 ft (70 m) above the Capilano River.

8 Brackendale
MAP E2

The community is best known for the bald eagles that winter in the nearby 3-sq-mile (7.8-sq-km) Brackendale Eagles Provincial Park, but the ocean and the river location here make this small town a very popular place for rafting and canoeing.

Juvenile bald eagle in Brackendale

9 Richmond
MAP B3 ■ www.richmond nightmarket.com

BC's fourth-largest city is making waves as a multicultural foodie destination. The Richmond Night Market from May till October, and the International Buddhist Temple (see p63) are well worth traveling for.

10 University of British Columbia

MAP A2 ■ 604 822 2211 ■ www. ubc.ca ■ Gardens: open daily; 604 822 4208; www.botanicalgarden. ubc.ca; adm

A lovely mix of historic and modern architecture, the buildings of BC's oldest university are complemented by diverse gardens. Stroll around the traditional Japanese Nitobe Memorial Garden, or navigate suspended walkways high up in the tree canopy at the Botanical Garden.

A DRIVE ALONG THE SEA-TO-SKY HIGHWAY

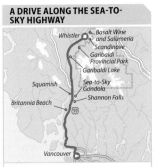

▶ MORNING

Start your day heading north from **Vancouver** on the Sea-to-Sky Highway, which is officially known as Highway 99. Tiny Britannia Beach and its Mine Museum make an interesting first stop. Shannon Falls, 4.5 miles (7 km) further on, is well worth the ten minutes on foot from the parking area off the highway. Continue driving on the dramatic coastal road to **Squamish** and take the ten-minute **Sea-to-Sky Gondola** to access summit trails, a suspension bridge, and sweeping views. Have lunch at one of the three great restaurants at Summit Lodge (604 892 2550), 2,900 ft (885 m) above Howe Sound.

AFTERNOON

After lunch, continue your journey north toward **Whistler** (see p101). Make sure to leave time for the renowned Garibaldi Provincial Park and its namesake turquoise lake; there are five access points to the park between Squamish and Pemberton, all with parking for various trailheads. A short final drive through the classic BC backcountry brings you to **Whistler** and its famous ski resort, **Whistler Blackcomb** (see p105), where you can spend as many hours or days as your itinerary allows. Book relaxing spa treatments at **Scandinave** (see p45) or take to one of the championship golf courses found nearby. An indulgent dinner at the excellent restaurant, **Basalt Wine and Salumeria** (see p106), will make a perfect end to your day.

See map on pp100–101

Best Green Spaces

1 Lighthouse Park
MAP A1 ■ Marine Dr & Beacon Ln, West Vancouver ■ 604 925 7275 ■ www.westvancouver.ca
Giant ferns and huge boulders are signatures of this waterfront park. Quiet trails lead through the area's last stand of old-growth trees.

2 Pacific Spirit Regional Park
MAP A2 ■ W 16th Ave at Blanca St ■ 604 224 5739 ■ www.metro vancouver.org
Over 45 miles (73 km) of trails snake through a stretch of thick rain forest, and along bogs and cliffs in this park.

3 VanDusen Botanical Garden
MAP B2 ■ 5151 Oak St ■ 604 257 8463 ■ Adm ■ www.vandusen garden.org
Secluded nooks and crannies can still be found at this world-famous garden with seasonal flower displays.

4 Cypress Provincial Park
MAP E3 ■ Top of Cypress Bowl Rd, West Vancouver ■ 604 926 5612 ■ www.bcparks.ca
Cypress Mountain, in the park, offers sports galore and great views as far as Mount Baker in Washington State.

5 Queen Elizabeth Park
MAP B2 ■ W 33rd Ave & Cambie St ■ 604 873 7000 ■ www.vancouver.ca
Located 499 ft (152 m) above sea level, this park (see p49) is the highest point in Vancouver. It offers a conservatory, lovely gardens, and splendid views.

6 Boundary Bay Regional Park
MAP F4 ■ Boundary Bay Rd, Tsawwassen ■ 604 520 6442 ■ www.metrovancouver.org
Beachcombers, horseback riders, and birders frequent this pretty oceanside park throughout the year.

7 Mount Seymour Provincial Park
MAP C1 ■ 1700 Mt Seymour Rd, North Vancouver ■ 604 986 2261 ■ www.bcparks.ca
Skiers and snowshoers relish the snow and gentle slopes in winter. In summer, hikers come for the views.

8 George C. Reifel Migratory Bird Sanctuary
MAP E4 ■ 5191 Robertson Rd, Delta ■ 604 946 6980 ■ Adm ■ www.reifel birdsanctuary.com
Some 60,000 birds visit this huge site on Westham Island yearly. View the wetlands from platforms and hides.

9 West Dyke Recreational Trail
MAP A3 ■ www.richmond.ca
Enjoy awe-inspiring views of Sturgeon Banks, which attracts 1.4 million birds annually, at this 3.5-mile (5.5-km) trail.

10 Deer Lake Park
MAP C2 ■ Canada Way & Sperling Ave, Burnaby ■ 604 294 7450 ■ www.burnaby.ca
This park has plenty of wildlife, trails, picnic spots, a playground, various art centers, a restaurant, and the open-air Burnaby Village Museum.

Conservatory at Queen Elizabeth Park

Adventure Sports

Mountain biking in Squamish

1 Mountain Biking
Mountain Biking BC: www.mountainbikingbc.ca

The 93-mile (150-km) Sea-to-Sky trail stretches from Squamish to D'Arcy. Find trail maps on Mountain Biking BC's website.

2 Backcountry Skiing & Snowboarding
Mountain Skills Academy: www.mountainskillsacademy.com

Ski or snowboard near the resort with a guide in the Sea to Sky area mountains. Basic experience required.

3 Kayaking Tours
West Coast Expeditions: 250 338 2511; www.westcoastexpeditions.com

Take a multiple-day kayaking tour for both experienced and novice adventurers around the stunning coastline.

4 Paragliding
iParaglide: www.iparaglide.com

Learn to be airborne on a tandem flight with a certified teacher. Coastal winds ensure breathtaking heights.

5 Rock Climbing
Squamish Rock Guides: 604 892 7816; www.squamishrockguides.com

Squamish is one of the top climbing areas in North America. You'll have to brave Stawamus Chief, a formidable cliff rising 2,303 ft (702 m).

6 Windsurfing
Squamish Windsports Society: www.squamishwindsports.com

Windsurfers converge at the mouth of the Squamish River on Howe Sound. Squamish Windsports Society operates the sailing park and the rescue service, and charges a sailing fee.

7 Diving
Diving Locker: 604 736 2681; www.divinglocker.ca

Find marine life, diving spots, and artificial reefs at Howe Sound's many dive sites. The Diving Locker offers charters, lessons, and equipment.

8 Whitewater Rafting
Chilliwack River Rafting: www.chilliwackriverrafting.com

With over a dozen rapids to navigate, the Chilliwack River is great for rafting. Stop at a hidden waterfall for lunch while keeping an eye on the riverbanks for black bears and other wildlife.

Rafting on the Chilliwack River

9 Skydiving
Abbotsford Skydive Center: 604 327 5867; www.vancouver-skydiving.bc.ca

The view of the Fraser Valley at 3,000 ft (915 m) is amazing. First-jump tandem lessons are available from Abbotsford Skydive Center.

10 Glacier Skiing
Whistler Blackcomb: 604 967 8950; www.whistlerblackcomb.com

Horstman Glacier (see p34) offers 128 acres of skiing and incomparable views year-round.

See map on pp100–103

Hiking Trails

1 Tunnel Bluffs
MAP E3

A 5.3-mile (8.5-km) route starting at Tunnel Point past Lions Bay, it follows old logging roads and steep trails with viewpoints of Howe Sound on the way.

2 Dog Mountain
MAP F3 ■ www.metro vancouver.org

Best done in snowshoes during winter, this 3-mile (5-km) trail in Mount Seymour Provincial Park offers a bird's eye view of Vancouver from the top.

3 Quarry Rock
MAP F3 ■ www.lynncanyon.ca

A relatively easy 2.5-mile (4-km) climb up and down, this trail winds through wooden stairs, bridges and thick forest cover. It ends on a rocky outcrop with incredible views of Deep Cove.

4 Cypress Falls
MAP E3 ■ www.west vancouver.ca

Winding through Cypress Fall Park, this is a 1.9-mile (3-km) round-trip trek through rain forests and Cypress Creek. Two awe-inspiring waterfalls await you at this hidden gem.

5 Grouse Grind
MAP E3 ■ www.grouse mountain.com

With its trailhead at the base of Grouse Mountain, this steep one-way hike is

Stunning forests along Grouse Grind

not for the faint hearted. It involves 2,830 steps and a thrilling 2,800-ft (853-m) elevation gain. Hikers have to take the Skyride gondola back down.

The dazzling Garibaldi Lake

6 Garibaldi Lake
MAP E2 ■ www.bcparks.ca; pre-book to camp

Take your camping gear along on this hike. The view of the jewel-colored lake crowned by snowy peaks is well worth the 11-mile (18-km) round trip.

7 Stawamus Chief
MAP E3 ■ www.explore squamish.com

Climbing along chains and ropes on this three-hour round trip may be intimidating, but you'll be rewarded with a stunning view of the Howe Sound.

8 Brandywine Falls
MAP E2 ■ www.bcparks.ca

Located close to Whistler, these falls are easily accessible along a half-mile (1-km) flat path in Brandywine Falls Provincial Park.

9 Killarney Lake Loop
MAP E3 ■ www.tourismbowen island.com

Bring the kids along this easy but magical 2.5-mile (4-km) hike through rain forests and a pretty little lake.

10 Buntzen Lake Loop
MAP F3 ■ www.buntzenlake.ca

This popular four-hour loop snakes around the Buntzen Lake Reservoir, and has an easy, mostly shaded, trail.

Restaurants

 Caramba!
MAP F1 ▪ 12–4314 Main St, Town Plaza, Whistler ▪ 604 938 1879 ▪ $$

This relaxed restaurant encourages families to share wood-oven pizza, calamari, and rotisserie meats.

 Fergie's Café
MAP E2 ▪ 70002 Squamish Valley Rd, Squamish ▪ 604 898 1537 ▪ Closed D ▪ $$

Located on the scenic Squamish river, Fergie's is known for its epic brunch menu with a focus on locally sourced ingredients.

3 Workshop Vegetarian Café
MAP E3 ▪ 296 Pemberton Ave, North Vancouver ▪ 604 973 0163 ▪ Closed Sat & Sun ▪ $

This quirky Japanese-inspired café offers tasty healthy fare. It's great for coffee, cake or the signature ramen.

4 Salmon House on the Hill
MAP B1 ▪ 2229 Folkstone Way, West Vancouver ▪ 604 926 3212 ▪ $$$

Perched in the North Shore hills, this restaurant is known for its flavorful green alderwood-grilled BC salmon.

5 The Galley Patio & Grill
MAP E4 ▪ 1300 Discovery St ▪ 604 222 1331 ▪ Closed winter ▪ $

With one of the best patios in Vancouver, this outdoor beachside res-taurant offers pub-style food and great craft beer.

6 Anton's Pasta Bar
MAP C2 ▪ 4260 Hastings St, Burnaby ▪ 604 299 6636 ▪ $

A great spot to enjoy large portions of tasty pasta. Expect lines but its worth the wait.

PRICE CATEGORIES
For a three-course meal for one with half a bottle of wine (or equivalent meal), taxes and extra charges.

$ under $35 $$ $35–85 $$$ over $85

 Honey's Doughnuts
MAP F3 ▪ 4373 Gallant Ave, North Vancouver ▪ 604 929 4988 ▪ Closed D ▪ $$

A great place for breakfast and lunch, Honey's has gained a reputation for some of the best donuts in the area.

8 The Beach House at Dundarave Pier
MAP B1 ▪ 150 25th St, West Vancouver ▪ 604 922 1414 ▪ $$

Sit on the deck of this 1912 house, choose a glass of wine from the long list, and enjoy West Coast cuisine.

9 Bar Oso
MAP F1 ▪ 150-4222 Village Green, Whistler ▪ 604 962 4540 ▪ Closed L ▪ $$$

Enjoy tapas, charcuterie, and hand-crafted cocktails at this chic spot.

10 Araxi
MAP F1 ▪ 4222 Village Sq, Whistler ▪ 604 932 4540 ▪ $$$

Local produce is served with a Pacific Northwest slant at this vibrant spot. Try the oysters, salmon or lamb confit.

Elegant dining room at Araxi

See map on p100–101

Streetsmart

**Sunny Maple Tree Square
in Gastown**

Getting Around

Arriving by Air

Vancouver International Airport (YVR) is located in Richmond, 9 miles (15 km) from downtown Vancouver. International and domestic flights arrive at the Main Terminal.

The cheapest and quickest way to get to downtown Vancouver is on the rapid transit Canada Line (a one-time $5 AddFare applies to your journey). It operates from 5am to 1am and takes 30 minutes to reach downtown. If you require transport when it's not running, an Uber or Lyft taxi is your best option.

Courtesy hotel shuttle pick-up and drop-off areas are outside of Arrivals on level 2 of the Main Terminal. Car rentals, taxis and public buses also operate from the airport.

Victoria International Airport (YYJ) is 15 miles (24 km) north of Victoria. The airport is serviced by several public buses (Nos. 87 and 88) and long-distance coaches. The **YYJ Airport Shuttle** departs every 30–60 minutes for major Victoria hotels. There are also taxis and car rentals.

Train Travel

The main hub for trains is **Pacific Central Station** in downtown Vancouver. **VIA Rail** trains arrive from various destinations all over Canada. The **Amtrak Cascades** route connects Vancouver to Eugene and Portland in Oregon, and to Seattle in Washington with daily trains.

Long-Distance Bus Travel

Greyhound buses arrive from the US at Pacific Central Station, as does the **BC Ferries Connector** bus from Victoria.

Driving

Most of the major car rental companies, such as **Avis**, **Hertz**, and **Budget**, have booths at Vancouver and Victoria airports. In Vancouver airport they are located on the ground floor of the parking garage and in Victoria airport you will find them in the arrivals hall. Insurance coverage for drivers is mandatory in BC. Check your policy to see if it covers a rental car (some credit cards include car insurance coverage).

Washington state's I-5 connects with Highway 99 at the BC border, leading to Vancouver and Whistler. BC's main Canada–US border crossing is the International Peace Arch in Blaine, Washington.

A good map, smart-phone, or GPS navigation device is essential, especially in Vancouver. Highways 1 and 99 can be very busy at rush hour, and there are no freeways bypassing the city core. Speed limits are posted. Right-hand turns on red lights are legal throughout BC unless otherwise stated. If you are driving in downtown Vancouver, note that a section of Granville Street is closed to private vehicles; signs direct you to side streets.

Ferries

BC Ferries connects Vancouver with Victoria, the Gulf Islands, and Nanaimo. **Hullo** operates a high-speed ferry for foot passengers only from downtown Vancouver to Nanaimo. Cruise ships dock at Canada Place (see pp14–15). Pleasure boats dock at the many marinas; visit the **Ahoy British Columbia** website for details.

Public Transportation

TransLink operates the public transit network in Vancouver. Safety and hygiene measures, ticket information, maps, and more can be obtained from its website. To travel, you can tap your credit or debit card, or buy a reloadable Compass Card, a Compass Wearable, a DayPass, or a Compass Ticket, which covers all transport on the network for a period of 90 minutes. Children under 12 years of age ride free.

Vancouver's SkyTrain is mainly an above-ground light rapid transit system. It includes the Expo Line, Millennium Line, and the Canada Line, which has 16 stations and links downtown to Vancouver airport and Richmond. The SkyTrain system has three fare zones, but on week-days after 6:30pm, and at the weekend and holidays, it reverts to one zone.

TransLink bus routes extend across much of Greater Vancouver. Bus-only travel is a one-zone fare. Bus drivers do not sell tickets; tap in with a credit, debit or Compass Card or Ticket or pay the exact cash fare when boarding. You will need to tap your card again or get another Compass Ticket to switch to the SkyTrain or the SeaBus, which is a catamaran that crosses the harbor in a short 12-minute trip.

Much of Vancouver Island is covered by **BC Transit**. There are two fare zones, and children under the age of 12 travel free.

Taxis

You can flag down cabs in central Vancouver, but you will need to phone for a taxi in Greater Vancouver and on Vancouver Island. **Bluebird Cabs** is one of the companies that operates in Victoria. Uber and Lyft also operate around Vancouver and Victoria.

Watertaxis

Aquabus and **False Creek Ferries** have various stops around False Creek and Granville Island.

Seaplanes

Operated by **Harbour Air**, seaplanes cut the journey time between Vancouver and Vancouver Island (Victoria or Nanaimo) down to 30 minutes. They also run services to Whistler, the Sunshine Coast, and other local destinations.

Cycling

Vancouver's bike rental scheme **Mobi** is ideal if you want to ride for 30 minutes or less. To cruise around for the day, or bike on Vancouver Island, hire from one of the many bike rental companies.

Try Vancouver's **Spokes Bicycle Rentals** or **Pedaler** in Victoria.

Cyclists must follow the same rules of the road as drivers. Bikes may not be ridden on sidewalks, and wearing a helmet is mandatory. Bikes are allowed on Vancouver's SkyTrain and SeaBus in non-peak hours. Many buses in both cities offer bike racks.

Walking

Walking is the best way to explore downtown Vancouver and Victoria, and streets are, for the main part, very safe. The Seawall (see p12) is a fantastic walking path around Stanley Park and on toward False Creek Inlet. In Victoria, the Inner Harbour (see p28) promenade has views of historic buildings and the harbor.

DIRECTORY

ARRIVING BY AIR

Vancouver International Airport (YVR)
w yvr.ca

Victoria International Airport (YYJ)
w victoriaairport.com

YYJ Airport Shuttle
w yyjairportshuttle.com

TRAIN TRAVEL

Amtrak Cascades
w amtrakcascades.com

Pacific Central Station
c 1 888-842-7245

VIA Rail
w viarail.ca

LONG-DISTANCE BUS TRAVEL

BC Ferries Connector
w bcfconnector.com

Greyhound
w greyhound.com

DRIVING

Avis
w avis.ca

Budget
w budget.ca

Hertz
w hertz.ca

FERRIES

Ahoy British Columbia
w ahoybc.com

BC Ferries
w bcferries.com

Hullo
w hullo.com

PUBLIC TRANSPORTATION

BC Transit
w bctransit.com

TransLink
w translink.ca

TAXIS

Bluebird Cabs
w taxicab.com

WATERTAXIS

Aquabus
w theaquabus.com

False Creek Ferries
w granvilleisland
ferries.bc.ca

SEAPLANES

Harbour Air
w harbourair.com

CYCLING

Mobi
w mobibikes.ca

Pedaler
w thepedaler.ca

Spokes Bicycle Rentals
w spokesbicycle
rentals.com

Practical Information

Passports and Visas

For entry requirements, including visas, consult your nearest Canadian embassy or check the visa section of the **Canadian Government** website. Citizens of the US, EU, UK, and British Commonwealth countries do not require visas, but must apply to enter in advance for the Electronic Travel Authorization (eTA) via the government website. Visitors may remain in Canada for up to six months. The Government of Canada's **Travel and Tourism** website has further detailed information on entry regulations.

Government Advice

Now more than ever, it is important to consult both your and the Canadian government's advice before traveling. The **UK Foreign, Commonwealth & Development Office**, the **US Department of State**, the **Australian Department of Foreign Affairs and Trade**, and the **Government of Canada** offer the latest information on security, health, and local regulations.

Customs Information

You can find information on the laws relating to goods and currency taken in or out of Canada on the **Canada Border Services Agency** website. The rules are fairly complex so it's important to read up before you travel. In general, do not try to bring fresh fruit, vegetables, meat, dairy products, live animals, plants, or firearms into Canada without obtaining authorization in advance. Limited amounts of alcohol and tobacco may be imported into the country duty-free by visitors who are 19 years of age or older. Cannabis is legal in Canada but it is illegal to bring it in or take it out of the country. Upon entry into Canada, all visitors must declare any cash amount equal to or more than C$10,000.

Insurance

We recommend taking out a comprehensive insurance policy covering theft, loss of belongings, medical care, cancellations, and delays, and read the small print carefully.

Health

Canada has a world-class healthcare system, and residents have access to free health care through health insurance plans. Canada does not, however, have reciprocal health agreements with other countries, so it is important to take out health insurance prior to visiting.

For minor ailments, pharmacies offer a good source of advice and medicinal supplies, and walk-in clinics are available in Vancouver. In smaller communities, the emergency room of the closest hospital is the best option.

In Vancouver, Victoria, and Whistler, emergency treatment is available 24 hours a day. In rural areas, however, operating hours may vary. Consider going to an urgent care center for minor emergencies: the urgent care center at **UBC Hospital**, located 8 miles (12 km) from downtown Vancouver, is open every day from 8am to 10pm.

For information regarding COVID-19 vaccination requirements, consult government advice. No other vaccinations are required for Canada. Unless otherwise stated, tap water is safe to drink.

There are dangers associated with wilderness expeditions to the backcountry. Seek local advice about wild animals (including cougars and bears), dangerous plants (including poison ivy), and insects (including blackflies and mosquitoes), and always boil water that might be unsafe to drink.

Smoking, Alcohol, and Drugs

In BC, smoking, vaping and e-cigarettes are banned on all modes of transportation, in all public places, and workspaces, including within 16 ft (5 m) of doors and windows.

The legal limit for drivers in Canada is 80 mg of alcohol per 100 ml of blood or 0.08 per cent BAC (blood alcohol content). This is roughly equivalent to a small glass of wine or a pint of regular-strength beer.

Recreational use of cannabis is legal in Canada, for those aged 19 or older. You are limited to carrying up to 30 grams of dried cannabis in public, and smoking is permitted outside. While you can legally take cannabis from province to province within Canada, taking it into another country can result in prosecution. Possession of certain illegal drugs may entail heavy fines and possibly jail time.

ID

There is no requirement for visitors to carry ID, but due to occasional checks you may be asked to show your passport. If you don't have it with you, you may be asked to present the original document within 24 hours. Bars, clubs, and liquor stores regularly ask for two types of ID in BC (one with a photo and one with just your name).

Personal Security

Vancouver and Vancouver Island are relatively safe places to visit, but petty crime does take place. Pickpockets work known tourist areas and busy streets. Use your common sense, keep valuables in a safe place, and be alert to your surroundings.

If you have anything stolen, report the crime as soon as possible at the nearest police station. Get a copy of the crime report to claim on your insurance. Contact your embassy or consulate immediately if your passport is stolen or in the event of a serious crime or accident.

Various helplines are available to call in a crisis. Call the **emergency number** if you need an ambulance, fire brigade, or urgent police services. If it is not an emergency but you need to speak to the police, telephone either the **Victoria Police** or the **Vancouver Police**, depending on your location.

As a rule, Canadians are very accepting of all people, regardless of their race, gender or sexuality. In 2005, Canada became the fourth country in the world, and the first in the Americas, to legalize same-sex marriage. Today, Vancouver has one of the largest LGBTQ+ populations in Canada. If you do feel unsafe in the city, look for the **VPD Safe Space** multicoloured logo in windows of businesses, which indicates a place of refuge from where you can call the police.

First Nations, Métis, and Inuit peoples in Canada have faced historic prejudice and discrimination, with suffrage only being extended to Indigenous people in 1960. Today, a disproportionate number of Indigenous women go missing or are murdered each year. **Hope for Wellness** offers immediate mental health counselling and crisis intervention to all Indigenous peoples across Canada.

DIRECTORY

PASSPORTS AND VISAS

Canadian Government
w cic.gc.ca/english/visit/visas.asp

Travel and Tourism
w travel.gc.ca

GOVERNMENT ADVICE

Australian Department of Foreign Affairs and Trade
w smartraveller.gov.au

Government of Canada
w canada.ca

UK Foreign, Commonwealth & Development Office
w gov.uk/foreign-travel-advice

US Department of State
w travel.state.gov

CUSTOMS INFORMATION

Canada Border Services Agency
w cbsa-asfc.gc.ca

HEALTH

UBC Hospital
c 604 822 7121

PERSONAL SECURITY

Emergency Number
c 911

Hope for Wellness
w hopeforwellness.ca

Vancouver Police
c 604 717 3321

Victoria Police
c 250 995 7654

VPD Safe Space
w vpdsafeplace.com

Travelers with Specific Requirements

Most attractions, lodgings, and transportation agencies can accommodate people with disabilities if you make your specific requirements known at the time of booking. All public buildings provide wheelchair access and suitable toilet facilities, and almost all street corners have dropped kerbs. Car rental companies can provide vehicles with hand controls at no extra charge, if booked ahead. All public transportation is accessible and passengers with reduced mobility may be entitled to priority boarding and free travel for one companion. Check the Canadian Transportation Agency (**CTA**) website for details. Provincial tourist offices are the top source of information on accessible hotels, motels, and attractions. You can find further information on the **Access to Travel** website. The **CNIB Foundation** offers helpful information and advice for blind and partially sighted travelers.

Time Zone

Vancouver and Vancouver Island are on Pacific Time (eight hours behind GMT). Daylight Saving Time begins in mid-March when clocks are turned forward one hour, and ends in early November when clocks are turned back one hour.

Money

The unit of currency is the Canadian dollar (CAD or C$). Most establishments accept major credit, debit, and prepaid currency cards. Contactless payments are widely accepted, however, it is worth carrying some cash for smaller items, tips and transportation tickets.

Waiters expect to be tipped 15 to 20 per cent of the total bill, hotel porters and housekeeping should be given $2–3 per bag or day, and taxi drivers appreciate 10 to 15 per cent of the fare.

Electrical Appliances

Canada uses a 110-volt, 60-cycle electrical system. Electrical sockets are type A and B, fitting two- or three-pronged plugs.

Cell Phones and Wi-Fi

Local SIM cards can be used in compatible phones and can be bought from local providers. US residents can upgrade their domestic cell phone plan to extend to Canada.

Free Wi-Fi spots are generally available in airports, libraries, and most hotels. Cafés and restaurants permit the use of their Wi-Fi on the condition that you make a purchase. Note that phone signal is patchy along mountain roads.

Postal Services

Post offices and service counters in Vancouver and on Vancouver Island are operated by **Canada Post**. Check its website to find the nearest outlet. Stamps can be bought from post offices, and some supermarkets, drug stores, and even corner grocery stores. Allow one to two weeks when sending mail overseas. Parcels may take upward of two weeks.

Weather

The temperate coastal climate of Vancouver and Vancouver Island is at its best April to November. Rain falls intermittently November to March, but low season is a good time for storm-watching.

In the city and along the coast, winter temperatures rarely drop below freezing, but are far lower high up in the mountains. Whistler sees an annual snowfall of 39 ft (11.9 m).

Opening Hours

Situations can change quickly and unexpectedly. Always check before visiting attractions and hospitality venues for up-to-date opening hours and booking requirements.

Most shops are open from 9am to 6pm Monday to Saturday (often later on Thursday evenings). Department stores and shops in malls and retail districts may stay open to 9pm Monday to Saturday, and open on Sunday from 11am or noon to 5pm. Many shops close on January 1, July 1, Labor Day, Thanksgiving, and December 25. Some attractions close on Mondays, and on public holidays many places close early or all day.

Visitor Information

Destination Vancouver (see p15), Tourism Victoria, Vancouver Island Travel, and Destination BC all have tourist information centers across the region, as well as websites that are an excellent first stop when planning your trip. Another useful source of information is the City of Vancouver website.

A helpful app to download is what3words. This is a geocode system that divides the world into 3 m x 3 m squares and pinpoints your exact location – ideal when exploring the region's remote areas.

Responsible Tourism

One of the world's most sustainable cities, Vancouver is striving to operate on 100 per cent renewable energy by 2050. There are simple ways visitors can help towards this greener future: consider cycling, walking, and using public transportation when you can; and embrace locally sourced cuisine.

Visitors should also acknowledge the Indigenous history of the land and be respectful of local traditions. Turn off your cell phone and only take photographs if permitted at sacred sights.

Tours

Walking tours are a great way to discover the city and surrounding area. Take a walk with Tours by Locals or learn about Vancouver's Chinatown with tour guides from the Chinese Canadian Museum (see p40). Forbidden Vancouver offers tours

about the Prohibition and the darker side of the city's history, while Discover the Past brings Victoria's history to life.

Big Bus Victoria runs a seasonal double decker hop-on hop-off tour of Victoria and also provides a shuttle to Butchart Gardens (see p94). West Coast Sightseeing has a daily shuttle from Vancouver to Whistler and operates a year-round city bus tour. It also operates a hop-on-hop-off service.

Language

English is the official language in BC. Although French is Canada's other official language, it isn't widely spoken in BC.

Taxes and Refunds

A 5 percent Goods and Services Tax (GST) is levied on most goods and services, as well as an additional 7 per cent Provincial Sales Tax (PST). There are also additional taxes on tourist lodging.

Non-resident visitors to Canada are unable to claim tax rebates for goods and services purchased in the country.

Accommodation

The Vancouver area offers a variety of accommo-dation, from luxury hotels to B&Bs and budget hostels. A comprehensive list of options can be found on the Destination BC web-site. Peak rates apply from April to December. In BC, accommodation is taxed with 8 per cent provincial hotel room tax. Most hotels are also required to add an additional 3 per

cent tourism tax on hotel rooms (this applies in Victoria, Whistler, Tofino, Ucluelet, and Vancouver).

DIRECTORY

TRAVELERS WITH SPECIFIC REQUIREMENTS

Access to Travel
W accesstotravel.gc.ca

CNIB Foundation
W cnib.ca

CTA
W otc-cta.gc.ca

POSTAL SERVICES

Canada Post
W canadapost.ca

VISITOR INFORMATION

City of Vancouver
W vancouver.ca

Destination BC
W hellobc.com

Tourism Victoria
W tourismvictoria.com

Vancouver Island Travel
W vancouverisland.travel

what3words
W what3words.com

TOURS

Big Bus Victoria
W bigbusvictoria.com

Discover the Past
W discoverthepast.com

Tours by Locals
W toursbylocals.com

West Coast Sightseeing
W westcoastsightseeing.com

Places to Stay

PRICE CATEGORIES
For a standard double room per night with breakfast (if included), taxes, and extra charges

$ under $150 $$ $150–350 $$$ over $350

Vancouver Luxury and Boutique Hotels

St. Regis Hotel
MAP K3 ■ 602 Dunsmuir St ■ 604 681 1135 ■ www.stregishotel.com ■ $$
In an ideal location for shopping and clubbing, the St. Regis offers rooms with balconies, oversized tubs, and stellar views of the harbor, city, and mountains. Breakfast is complimentary.

The Listel Hotel
MAP J3 ■ 1300 Robson St ■ 604 684 8461 ■ www.thelistelhotel.com ■ $$$
A beautiful boutique hotel with rooms that display works by local artists. The onsite restaurant, Forage (see p81), serves excellent farm-to-table dishes; the brunch is particularly good.

Metropolitan Hotel
MAP K3 ■ 645 Howe St ■ 604 687 1122 ■ www.metropolitan.com ■ $$$
Every step is taken to maximize the comfort of guests, with European down duvets, marble bathrooms, an indoor pool, and health club. It also houses the delightful Diva at the Met restaurant (see p81).

Opus Hotel
MAP J5 ■ 322 Davie St ■ 604 642 6787 ■ www.opushotel.com ■ $$$
This stylish boutique hotel is a Yaletown trendsetter. Take advantage of the wonderful on-site Italian restaurant, and relax in the sophisticated lounge.

Rosewood Hotel Georgia
MAP K3 ■ 801 W Georgia St ■ 604 682 5566 ■ www.rosewoodhotels.com ■ $$$
Treat yourself to a stay at this elegant and legendary retreat. It first opened as the Hotel Georgia in 1927, and has been beautifully restored. The Hawksworth restaurant is exemplary. On warm summer evenings, dine out on the hotel's garden terrace.

Shangri-La Hotel
MAP J3 ■ 1128 W Georgia St ■ 604 689 1120 ■ www.shangri-la.com ■ $$$
In the heart of downtown, this opulent hotel offers luxury rooms featuring marble-furnished bathrooms with bath tubs. Some of the rooms have balconies and kitchens.

Wedgewood Hotel & Spa
MAP J3 ■ 845 Hornby St ■ 604 689 7777 ■ www.wedgewoodhotel.com ■ $$$
Founded by hotelier Eleni Skalbania, this boutique hotel has European flair. The place caters to those who prefer their accommodation upscale, verging on exclusive. Free bicycle rentals are available too.

Westin Bayshore
MAP J2 ■ 1601 Bayshore Dr ■ 604 682 3377 ■ www.marriott.com ■ $$$
Sitting on Coal Harbour, between Stanley Park and downtown, this hotel has comfortable rooms, and offers guests the best of both worlds: nature and outdoor activities. Its close proximity to the downtown hustle and bustle makes it an ideal urban retreat.

Vancouver Business and Suite Hotels

Best Western Plus Chateau Granville
MAP J4 ■ 1100 Granville St ■ 604 669 7070 ■ www.chateaugranville.com ■ $$
A frequent choice for out-of-towners seeking a good location and value for money, this 15-story hotel offers mainly one-bedroom suites, but has some smaller, standard rooms as well. Suites come with microwaves.

The Burrard
MAP J4 ■ 1100 Burrard St ■ 604 681 2331 ■ www.theburrard.com ■ $$
The charming rooms at this retro-style hotel have modern amenities such as Nespresso machines and mini-fridges. Perks include free bike rentals and treats for pets.

Residence Inn Vancouver Downtown
MAP J4 ■ 1234 Hornby St ■ 604 688 1234 ■ www.marriott.com ■ $$
Close to Yaletown and the Davie Street shopping area, this hotel's spacious

suites with kitchens and seating areas are a great option for an extended stay. There is an indoor pool, a gym, and complimentary breakfast.

Sunset Inn and Suites
MAP H4 ■ 1111 Burnaby St ■ 438 795 6650 ■ www. sunsetinn.com ■ $$
Found in a high-rise in the West End, this hotel's location is central but off the main thoroughfare, so it is quieter than some others. It is suitable for both short- and long-term stays. Breakfast and parking are complimentary.

Fairmont Waterfront
MAP K2 ■ 900 Canada Pl ■ 604 691 1991 ■ www. fairmont.com ■ $$$
Linked to the convention center by an enclosed walkway, this harborside property has an accessible rooftop garden, a 24-hour gym, an outdoor heated pool, and a stylish cocktail bar. Stay on the Fairmont Gold levels to enjoy additional service and amenities.

Georgian Court Hotel
MAP L4 ■ 773 Beatty St ■ 604 682 5555 ■ www. georgiancourthotel vancouver.com ■ $$$
Providing an excellent location for sports fans in town to take in a game (BC Place Stadium and Rogers Arena are mere minutes away), this well-appointed business and leisure hotel offers air-conditioned rooms and suites. There is also a 24-hour fitness center and an infrared sauna. Enjoy the on-site kitchen and bar, which features authentic Italian fare.

Pan Pacific Vancouver
MAP L2 ■ 300-999 Canada Pl ■ 604 662 8111 ■ www. panpacific.com ■ $$$
Soaring over the famous waterfront, the Pan's rooms and luxury suites provide spectacular views of the North Shore mountains. With the convention center located in the same complex, this is regarded as North America's premiere convention hotel.

Vancouver Mid-Priced Hotels

Blue Horizon Hotel
MAP J3 ■ 1225 Robson St ■ 604 688 1411 ■ www.bluehorizon hotel.com ■ $$
Gorgeous views abound in this contemporary hotel, as each room has wraparound windows as well as a balcony. Other amenities include a mini-fridge, a Nespresso machine, and bathrobes.

Century Plaza Hotel & Spa
MAP J4 ■ 1015 Burrard St ■ 604 687 0575 ■ www. century-plaza.com ■ $$
This hotel is a modest, good-value choice. The really big draw here is the European-style spa (see p45), which has an indoor pool and steam room, as well as many excellent treatments. There's also a convenient lounge and restaurant, and a cappuccino bar.

Granville Island Hotel
MAP H6 ■ 1253 Johnston St ■ 604 683 7373 ■ www.granville islandhotel.com ■ $$
With delightful rooms overlooking False Creek, this intimate hotel is located right on Granville Island. It features pretty wooden shutters, beamed ceilings, and sumptuous oversized bath tubs. Dine at the refined Dockside restaurant (see p88), or choose from the many excellent eateries situated nearby.

Moda Hotel
MAP K4 ■ 900 Seymour St ■ 604 683 4251 ■ www. modahotel.ca ■ $$
A good-value, boutique hotel in a heritage 1908 building, it beautifully blends old-world style with contemporary interiors. There is a choice of an Italian restaurant, cocktail bar, and also a sports bar on site.

Skwachàys Lodge
MAP L4 ■ 31 W Pender ■ 604 687 3589 ■ www. skwachays.com ■ $$
Celebrating the culture of the Indigenous peoples, this boutique hotel and art gallery has decorated rooms, and also a floor dedicated to offering subsidized housing for Indigenous artists. The Downtown Eastside location is on the edge of a rougher neighbourhood, so consider a taxi at night.

Sylvia Hotel
MAP G2 ■ 1154 Gilford St ■ 604 681 9321 ■ www. sylviahotel.com ■ $$
The West End's grande dame is a favorite for its relaxed yet sophisticated atmosphere and a really fabulous location right on English Bay. Some rooms are tiny, but the big draws include the lounge and restaurant overlooking the water. It's a pet-friendly hotel, and covered paid parking is available.

Vancouver B&Bs and Guesthouses

Barclay House B&B
MAP H3 ■ 1351 Barclay St
■ 604 605 1351 ■ www.
barclayhouse.com ■ $$
A perennial West End favorite, this classic 1904 home features two-room suites, attentive staff, a full three-course breakfast, cookies on arrival, in-room refrigerator and drinks, as well as free parking.

English Bay Inn
MAP G2 ■ 1968 Comox St
■ 604 683 8002 ■ www.
englishbayinn.com ■ $$
A West End hideaway with cozy antique furniture and air-conditioned en suite rooms. The full breakfast by the fireplace makes a pleasant start to the day.

O Canada House
MAP J3 ■ 1114 Barclay St
■ 604 688 0555 ■ www.
ocanadahouse.com ■ $$
Built in 1897, this lovely guesthouse reflects the early elegance of the West End, including a parlor with a fireplace. A gourmet breakfast, evening sherry, 24-hour pantry for guests, and free parking are available.

Vancouver Traveller B&B
MAP E4 ■ 2159 W 21st Ave ■ 604 375 6182
■ www.vancouver travellerbb.com ■ $$
Located less than a ten-minute drive from downtown Vancouver, this modern B&B has a cottage and rooms with hardwood floors and in-floor heating. Breakfast is complimentary and guests also have access to a communal kitchenette.

Victorian Hotel
MAP L3 ■ 514 Homer St
■ 604 681 6369 ■ www.
victorianhotel.ca ■ $$
Built in 1898 as one of the city's first guesthouses, this hotel has been very carefully restored to retain its Victorian-era ambience. The highlights include bay windows, high ceilings, antique furnishings, and hardwood floors. It offers a comfortable setting, with beautiful bathrooms and down duvets on the beds.

West End Guest House
MAP J3 ■ 1362 Haro St
■ 604 681 2889 ■ www.
westendguesthouse.com
■ $$
This pretty pink and grey 1906 Victorian inn in Stanley Park offers one- and two-bedroom suites. There is free parking and bike storage, and full hot breakfast is served daily.

Vancouver Budget Hotels

Hostelling International Vancouver Downtown
MAP H4 ■ 1114 Burnaby St ■ 604 684 4565 ■ www.
hihostels.ca ■ $
Shared and private rooms are offered in this friendly West End spot. There's free breakfast, and the shared kitchen can help with the other meals. Guests can relax on the lovely, sunny rooftop patio.

Kingston Hotel
MAP K4 ■ 757 Richards St ■ 604 684 9024
■ www.kingston.hotels-vancouver.net ■ $
Set in a relaxed 1910 heritage building, this hotel has private and shared baths, day and overnight storage, a TV lounge, sauna, and a good pub. The room rate includes an excellent continental breakfast. Guests can also relax by the fireplace in the lounge.

Samesun Vancouver
MAP J4 ■ 1018 Granville St ■ 604 682 8226 ■ www.
samesun.com ■ $
Choose from private en suite or dorm-style rooms at this centrally located hostel in the heart of the Entertainment District. Amenities include a shared kitchen, laundry, common room, and complimentary breakfast. There's a lively pub perfect for a beer in the evening.

West Coast Suites at UBC
MAP A2 ■ 5961 Student Union Blvd ■ 604 822 1000 ■ www.suitesatubc. com ■ $
From May to August, take your pick from 3,000 rooms at UBC's beautiful campus. Year-round, one-bedroom suites with kitchens are available. Each is spotlessly kept and offers free Wi-Fi. UBC is a city in itself, with many amenities on its grounds and nearby.

YWCA Hotel
MAP K5 ■ 733 Beatty St
■ 604 895 5830 ■ www.
ywcavan.org/hotel ■ $
Offering air-conditioned rooms to suit all types of travelers, including families, this is a secure, 12-story downtown high-rise. It has TVs in many of the rooms and is a great place for those who need their gym fix, with free admission to the fitness center. The hotel is fully wheelchair accessible.

Vancouver Island Hotels

Ocean Island Backpackers Inn, Victoria
MAP Q2 ■ 791 Pandora Ave ■ 250 385 1789 ■ www.oceanisland.com ■ $
Clean and comfortable, this hostel is in a historic building near Victoria's Inner Harbour. Dorms and private rooms are available. Breakfasts and dinners are included.

Robin Hood Inn and Suites, Victoria
MAP E6 ■ 136 Gorge Rd E ■ 250 388 4302 ■ www.robinhoodinn.ca ■ $
This motel offers spacious rooms and amenities such as Keurig coffee machines and a shuttle service. Free e-bike, kayak, and paddleboard rentals are also available.

Chateau Victoria Hotel & Suites, Victoria
MAP Q3 ■ 740 Burdett Ave ■ 250 382 4221 ■ www.chateauvictoria.com ■ $$
Located steps away from Victoria's Inner Harbour, this three-star business and leisure hotel features a rooftop restaurant and lounge that serves seasonal fare on the 18th floor.

Coast Bastion Hotel, Nanaimo
MAP D4 ■ 11 Bastion St ■ 250 753 6601 ■ www.coasthotels.com ■ $$
The best of Nanaimo's accommodation offerings, this smart hotel has great views across the waterfront. There's a business center, a great restaurant, a fitness room, and a gym.

Delta Victoria Ocean Pointe Resort, Victoria
MAP N2 ■ 100 Harbour Rd ■ 250 360 2999 ■ www.marriott.com ■ $$
Situated by the harbor, this hotel offers modern, quiet, and air-conditioned rooms. Amenities include an indoor pool, 24-hour gym, and sports courts.

Heathergate House, Victoria
MAP E6 ■ 122 Simcoe St ■ 250 383 0068 ■ www.victoria-vacationrentals.com ■ $$
Tucked away in a quiet, near-perfect spot, this hotel is close to Victoria's bustling Inner Harbour. The plush suites all have a private bath and kitchenette, and there is also a well-appointed garden cottage that easily sleeps four. A full English breakfast is included in the price of the rooms.

Huntingdon Manor Hotel, Victoria
MAP N4 ■ 330 Quebec St ■ 250 381 3456 ■ www.huntingdonmanor.com ■ $$
Charming and affordable, this hotel right by the Inner Harbour, offers a range of cozy rooms and stylish suites, including family suites for up to six people. The breakfast is included in the room rate.

Inn at Laurel Point, Victoria
MAP N3 ■ 680 Montreal St ■ 250 386 8721 ■ www.laurelpoint.com ■ $$
The spacious rooms here come with a view of Victoria's Inner Harbour. The Sunday brunch offered in the Aura Restaurant is excellent.

Magnolia Hotel & Spa, Victoria
MAP P3 ■ 623 Courtney St ■ 250 381 0999 ■ www.magnoliahotel.com ■ $$
This award-winning hotel wins over guests with its unbeatable location and service. The sumptuous rooms feature four-poster beds and marble bathrooms with deep soaker tubs.

Fairmont Empress Hotel, Victoria
MAP P4 ■ 721 Government St ■ 250 384 8111 ■ www.fairmont.com ■ $$$
One of the most famous hotels on the West Coast, Victoria's top luxury hotel offers small but elegant rooms. Make a reservation to take English-style tea in the glorious lobby (see p99), a pricey but noteworthy experience.

Oak Bay Beach Hotel, Victoria
MAP E6 ■ 1175 Beach Dr ■ 250 598 4556 ■ www.oakbaybeachhotel.com ■ $$$
The rooms at this hotel are elegant and feature large spa-like bathrooms, patios, and fireplaces. Guests can soak in the seaside mineral baths, or enjoy a drink at the pub.

Wickaninnish Inn, Tofino
MAP A4 ■ 500 Osprey Ln, Tofino ■ 250 725 3100 ■ www.wickinn.com ■ $$$
Perched dramatically on a rocky shelf overlooking Chesterman Beach, this highly acclaimed inn offers luxurious lodgings done in a modern West Coast style. With a great spa and gourmet restaurant, it's the perfect getaway spot.

For a key to hotel price categories see p116

Index

Acknowledgments

This edition updated by

Contributor Jacqueline Salomé
Senior Editors Dipika Dasgupta, Allison McGill
Senior Art Editor Vinita Venugopal
Project Editor Lucy Sara Kelly
Project Art Editor Ankita Sharma
Assistant Editor Abhidha Lakhera
Assistant Picture Research Administrator Manpreet Kaur
Project Picture Researcher Nishwan Rasool
Publishing Assistant Simona Velikova
Jacket Picture Researcher Kate Hockenhull
Jacket Designer Ankita Sharma
Cartographer Ashif
Cartography Manager Suresh Kumar
DTP Designer Tanveer Zaidi
Senior Production Editor Jason Little
Production Controller Kariss Ainsworth
Managing Editors Shikha Kulkarni, Beverly Smart, Hollie Teague
Senior Managing Art Editor Priyanka Thakur
Art Director Maxine Pedliham
Publishing Director Georgina Dee

DK would like to thank the following for their contribution to the previous editions: Constance Brissenden, Rachel Mills, Susanne Hillen, Helen Peters

The publisher would like to thank the following for their kind permission to reproduce their photographs:
Key: a-above; b-below/bottom; c-centre; f-far; l-left; r-right; t-top

Medina Café: Amy Ho 81c.

One Under – Urban Golf Club: 79cr.

Robert Harding Picture Library: Christian Kober 11clb; Peter Langer 40b.

Science World British Columbia: 26br, 27cr.

Score on Davie: 54t.

Steamworks Brewing: 72t.

SuperStock: age fotostock / Douglas Williams 25crb. 64cra.

Swirl Wine Store: 87cr.

The Pointe Restaurant: 97cl.

Toptable Group: Steveli 58tl, 59t, 81br, 107bl.

Collection of the Vancouver Art Gallery: Emily Carr Trust / Trevor Mills 10br, 40tl, 75cr; Founders' Fund / Trevor Mills 21tl.

Vancouver International Film Festival: 65clb.

Cover

Front and spine: **Getty Images/iStock:** RonTech2000

Back: **Alamy Stock Photo:** Michael Wheatley tl; **Getty Images/iStock:** RonTech2000 b, danbreckwoldt tr, Hadimor cla, MJ_Prototype crb.

Pull Out Map Cover

Getty Images/iStock: RonTech2.

All other images © Dorling Kindersley

For further information see:
www.dkimages.com

Commissioned Photography Gunter Marx, Alvin Kanak

First edition produced by International Book Productions Inc., Toronto

Penguin
Random
House

First edition 2006

First published in Great Britain by
Dorling Kindersley Limited
DK, One Embassy Gardens, 8 Viaduct
Gardens, London SW11 7BW, UK

The authorised representative in the EEA is
Dorling Kindersley Verlag GmbH. Arnulfstr.
124, 80636 Munich, Germany

Published in the United States by
DK Publishing, 1745 Broadway, 20th Floor,
New York, NY 10019, USA

Copyright © 2006, 2024 Dorling
Kindersley Limited

A Penguin Random House Company

24 25 26 27 10 9 8 7 6 5 4 3 2 1

The publishers cannot accept responsibility
for any consequences arising from the use
of this book, nor for any material on third
party websites, and cannot guarantee that
any website address in this book will be a
suitable source of travel information.

A CIP catalog record is available
from the British Library.

A catalog record for this book is available
from the Library of Congress.

ISSN 1479-344X
ISBN 978 0 2416 6856 6

Printed and bound in Malaysia

www.dk.com

As a guide to abbreviations in visitor information blocks: **Adm** = admission charge; **D** = dinner; **L** = lunch.

MIX
Paper | Supporting
responsible forestry
www.fsc.org **FSC™ C018179**

This book was made with Forest
Stewardship Council™ certified
paper – one small step in DK's
commitment to a sustainable future.
Learn more at
www.dk.com/uk/information/sustainability

Vancouver Selected Street Index

British Columbia Sight Index